NUBIAN
VOYAGER

Les Nubians
PRESENTS
from the Echos series

NUBIAN VOYAGER

Poetry and Music from the Urban Edge

EARTH AWARE
EDITIONS

ECHO

Nymphe de la mythologie
Gréco-romaine. Elle meurt de son
amour malheureux pour Narcisse,
sa voix seule lui survit, répétant les
dernières syllabes que l'on prononce.

✕ ✕✕✚✕✕ ✚ ✕ ✕ ✕✚✚✕✕ ✕ ✕

In Greek mythology, a nymph who,
spurned by Narcissus, pined away
until only her voice remained.

Qui sommes-nous
Sinon
Les Griots d'Hier
Les MCs d'Aujourd'hui
Et les ECHOS de Demain

We are the Griots of Yesterday
The MCs of Today
And the ECHOS of Tomorrow

Earth Aware Editions

17 Paul Drive, San Rafael, CA 94903
www.earthawareeditions.com
800.688.2218

Library of Congress Cataloging-in-Publication Data available.

ISBN 1-932771-76-X

10 9 8 7 6 5 4 3 2 1

Printed and bound in China by Palace Press International
www.palacepress.com

Cover Photograph by Luc Valigny & Piotr Sikora

Printed on acid-free paper.
Palace Press International, in
association with Global ReLeaf,
will plant two trees for each tree used in the manufacturing
of this book. Global ReLeaf is an international campaign by
American Forests, the nation's oldest nonprofit conservation
organization and a world leader in planting trees for
environmental restoration.

LE SPOKEN WORD.

Littéralement le Mot Parlé. Une expression poétique contemporaine, actuelle, urbaine et nouvelle dans sa forme.

Elle est issue du sol américain, fertile en contradictions et peut-être en raison de cela fertile pour ce qui est de créer des expressions artistiques nouvelles. Spoken Word, en français il faut dire Poésie Urbaine. Cette appellation définit au plus près ce qu'est le Spoken Word et correspond à une réalité française et francophone, celle d'une nouvelle vague d'expression poétique se redéfinissant au travers de l'inspiration de la rue, un vocabulaire nouveau, recyclé pour la beauté du son et du verbe, moulé dans des formes syntaxiques qui épousent les rythmes que nous vivons, les rythmes urbains. De là d'ailleurs l'union fréquente de la Poésie Urbaine avec la musique actuelle. Celle des sampleurs, des rythmes venus du hip hop et de tous les sons et de toutes les rythmiques nées ces vingt dernières années. Le Spoken Word, expression émergeant dans ce nouveau millénaire mais à mieux la regarder dernière descendante de l'art poétique de toutes les anciennes cultures orales. Spoken Word. Le Mot Parlé. L'oralité poétique confrontée à notre monde actuel. L'art se renouvelle au fil du temps, rien n'est perdu car tout se transforme.

Depuis les griots et toute la tradition poétique africaine d'expression orale, des scansions des pasteurs des églises noires, jusqu'aux Last Poets, Amiri Baraka, Aimé Césaire, en passant par le rap, cette tradition se perpétue, mieux elle mute au contact du monde pour reposer aujourd'hui par le Spoken Word dans la voix d'artistes tels que Saul Williams, pour le plus emblématique en passant par Jerry Quickley, Ursula Rucker, et dans celle de milliers d'autres qui enchantent à nouveau le verbe aux quatre coins du monde et qu'il nous faut entendre, entendre le Mot Parlé. Il nous faut même lire mais surtout écouter le Spoken Word pour saisir que les cultures anciennes ne meurent jamais mais ressuscitent dès que le vent permet à ses germes d'éclore en terrain fertile.

Et nous voici dans l'un de ces terrains fertiles. Porté comme la voix par une douce brise pour résonner dans Echos, *le voyageur Nubien*. *Echos* est une fenêtre ouverte sur ce nouveau monde poétique en plein essor, Echos est une trace pour rendre compte de la vigueur de la « tradition nouvelle » qu'est le Spoken Word, à la manière d'un journal de voyage. *Echos* est un reflet sonore et visuel de la voix de cette poésie et de ses poètes urbains, c'est un témoignage, celui de griots modernes qui disent le Spoken Word à l'unisson avec la richesse et les nuances de deux langues, le Français et l'Anglais. *Echos* est une photographie de cette nouvelle expression à découvrir d'urgence pour savoir que la poésie telle qu'elle nous fut apprise et que beaucoup pensaient vouée à rester confinée aux beaux livres reliés, dormant dans de riches bibliothèques poussiéreuses ou à de pieuses lectures raffinées dans de vieux salons dogmatisés, la poésie retrouve dans l'urbain sa raison d'être ; sa liberté, elle redevient parole dite et partagée, elle redevient notre, elle retourne enfin dans la voix de ceux qui nous ressemblent et qui disent par le Mot Parlé, le monde dans lequel nous vivons et celui dans lequel nous voudrions vivre. Le Spoken World. Le Monde Parlé. *Echos...*

Daniel Kline DuBois

otherwise known as Jomo Fulani Logsdon
otherwise known as The Dawn Breaker

SPOKEN WORD

A poetic vehicle that is contemporary, urban, a new form of expression.

It is a product of the American idiom, which is rich in contradictions and, perhaps for that reason, fertile ground for the creation of new artistic forms. Spoken word – the French would call it urban poetry. This phrase most accurately defines what spoken word is and corresponds to a French and French-speaking reality – that of a new wave of poetic expression that is redefined through street inspiration and a new vocabulary, recycled for the beauty of the sound and the language, molded into syntactical forms that fit the urban rhythms of our lives – which leads to the frequent union of urban poetry with modern music, the world of samplers, rhythms borrowed from hip hop, and all the other sounds and beats born within the last twenty years. Spoken word is a form of expression that is coming into its own in this new millennium, though it's actually the latest heir to the poetic art of oral expression inherent in all ancient cultures. Art renews itself over time; nothing is lost, because everything is transformed. Spoken word – poetry that defies the trappings of our modern world.

From the time of the griots – the keepers of the collective memories of their people and the guardians of the African poetic tradition of verbal expression – to the rhythmic delivery of the pastors of black churches, to the Last Poets, Amiri Baraka, Aimé Césaire, up to and including rap, the tradition continues, transformed upon contact with the contemporary world to bring us to today's spoken word, which finds its wings in the voices of such artists as Saul Williams (the most emblematic of all), Jerry Quickley, Ursula Rucker, and countless others who add their own personal magic to their language. And wherever we are in the world, we are compelled to listen to the spoken word – we can also read these words, of course, but it is the spoken word that ties us most intimately to our undying cultural roots: they are revived every time the seeds of our civilization sprout on fertile soil.

And we are now in the midst of fertile times. As a voice is carried by a soft breeze, so have the seeds of tradition been swept into the present, in the form of *Echos, The Nubian Voyager*. *Echos* is an open window onto this new poetic world in full expansion, a symbol that illustrates the strength of the new tradition that is the spoken word, in the style of a travelogue. *Echos* is an aural and visual expression of the voice of this poetry and of its urban poets, a monument to modern griots who chant the spoken word in unison, peppered with the richness and nuances of both French and English. *Echos* is a snapshot of this new form of expression, which urgently demands discovery so that we will recognize the fact that poetry – in the form it was taught to us, poetry that lived only in beautifully bound books tucked away in opulent, dust-covered libraries or in pious, refined readings in stern, stuffy halls – is rediscovering its reason for existence and its freedom, by taking up urban roots. It is again becoming the Word, spoken and shared, and it is again becoming our own, finally returning to the lips of those who speak for us and who tell us of both the world in which we live and the worlds that we dream of. The spoken word, the spoken world: *Echos...*

Daniel Kline DuBois

a.k.a. Jomo Fulani Logsdon
a.k.a. The Dawn Breaker

After a year and a half running the world east, west and north, I took a break south, seated in a felucca boat, on the Nile, in Aswan, NUBIA. And I feel great here. Time stops, frozen by a *"je-ne-sais-quoi"* mixed with a mystic energy coming from the earth, its historical scars and the healing waters that drown in each particle of this magic land.
Egypt. Nubia.
Myths and tales.
Isis and Osiris, and the temple of their everlasting love, the Philae temple. When the incarnated beauty and love Isis meets the powerful and the strong Osiris, even Goddesses and Gods get troubled. Seth killed Osiris and sliced him like a puzzle. Isis, sad and crushed, crossed the world searching for the pieces of the body. When she gathered every part, she brought her lover back to life with Anubis' help, just the necessary time to be pregnant of their only son: Horus.

Seated in the "King Of the Nile," I'm drinking "shaï" (traditional tea), and I remember Washington DC, Boston, Atlanta, San Francisco, Boulder, NYC, Paris, Yaoundé, Tokyo, London, Milan, Abidjan, Marseille, Bordeaux, all that amazing touring around the USA and beyond, and how many spirits and souls came to share with us. And the applause and the singing...it's so loud in my head that all Aswan and beyond can hear it. I feel so blessed and proud.

Seated in my Nubian felucca, with Captain Shahat and Captain Saïd, I see my little brothers struggling here for work, for life, in a new trendy and hype destination, promised to be the "Egyptian Riviera." Business, money, profits push the native Nubians out of their land, the Nubians are almost parked like native Indians in the U.S. or monkeys in a zoo, it's the same. The same shame. A tribe who made this part of Africa shine all around the world and ages, through space and time, is oppressed and stolen.
Anger, sadness, pain, and sorrows feed my inspiration, my creativity, my positive resistance.
A lot of things to write about.
A lot of stories and matters to sing about.

Seated in my Nubian felucca, the city's lights are so dazzling that I can even see Isis flying in the Nile's sky. Where are my hidden Nubian shining stars....

Seated in Captain Shahat's felucca, smoking an experimental and how designed Nubian spliff of tasty and pungent Nubian weed, I play with words in the darkness, trying to line up few ideas to introduce this collection concept.

LES NOUVEAUX GRIOTS/ The New Griots

2000: We're not so far from sci-fi writers' creations. Multimedia, communication are the challenge and the priority of our new century. Comas, letters, teardrops and cartoons, blood and fingerprints, smells and music, everything is recorded, codified and then disappears like invisible dusts and waves, in tubes and cables, invisibly linked to space.
More than ever, words, languages fight to stay alive and not being forgotten.
Words stay alive because of orality. I can even say that humanity stays alive because of orality.
The Griot. Memory of the family, the village. Witness and chronicler. Oral library. Sacred entertainer for the most important moments of your life, cheerfully for the best, spiritual and comforting for the worse. Ahmadou Hampate Ba, The Last Poets, Zora Neale Hurston, Amiri Baraka, Maya Angelou...showed us the way of this noble & ancestral discipline of free speech.

Here is the new generation of Griots. MCs, slammers, singers, urban poets, underground poets, modern poets...let's say poets.

Or Nouveaux Griots. Or ECHOS.

During Les Nubians U.S. Tour '99, we invited talented poets from all over the U.S. to join the show with their words, their vibes...and it was tremendous. We feel very honored to present you their creations and performances. Other poets from France, Poland, Senegal, Cameroon and Armenia joined the collective.

When it came to recording the project and following the tradition of poetry bare space, the poets wouldn't be influenced by the music. So we recorded all of them acapella, to keep their original breath and flow, tone, rhythm, each word carrying its own power, without salt nor sugar. Then I literally dove into each poem, to understand and feel their meanings and aura, so we could, with my fellow friend Mounir Belkhir (Producer of "Makeda" and more), dress those poems, set the proper universe for them to blossom and live. Each instrument and beat had been carefully chosen regarding the natural elements association needed (air, earth, water, fire). Sometimes, we took the freedom to create a few choruses, praying that the poets wouldn't find their work transformed. After months hidden in a basement studio, we were ready to submit the whole thing to the poets. We were so nervous...

That day in NYC, that special day in Paris, my bones were shaking...how would they feel it? I could breathe only at the end of the listening session. And that night, I cried with both joy and relief. We did it.

It was then time to persuade the music industry to pay attention to that art alternative. Makeda, the Queen of Sheba, sent us an army of angels to fight against dry hearts, deaf ears and hearts, castrating business laws, stupid thoughts, discouragement, stupid people, prejudice, words & music mobsters. The angels opened the path, as they know they are the ones whispering at the poets' ears....

This is the beginning of a Nouveaux Griots experience, echoes of souls, echoes of thoughts.

Seated in my white and green Nubian felucca, I remember Velska from Minneapolis saying, "I am a poet. You are a poet. She, he is a poet..."

Let's be the poets of our unconscious and buried existence and humanity:

> "We're the Griots of yesterday
> The MCs of today
> And the Echos of tomorrow..."

We offer you these flowers, those talented artists. May you look after them with love and attention.
All my prayers go to the Lord, Goddess Isis, my ancestors. May the Pharaohs stay in peace, and bring us peace.
I'm gonna sleep in my already missing Nubian felucca, my eyes into the Nile's sky.

We've been welcomed like real Nubian princesses.
Everywhere.
Thank you all.

H.

LES NUBIANS
OLU
LIP-SYNC FINALS TONITE
IN CONCERT
LES NUBIANS
TOWER RECORDS
TOP 25 ALWAYS ON SALE
ENTER TO WIN A TRIP
TO SEE ALANIS MORISSETTE
IN LONDON DETAILS INSIDE
HEAR & MEET
LES NUBIANS
HERE APR 6TH 7PM
COMEDY & SUPPER CLUB
22 OLD 97 S
23 CHARLES FEELGOOD
BETA BAND
24 LES NUBIANS
25 JOHN PAUL JONES
ZAP MAMA
THEATRE of the
LIVING ARTS
TONIGHT
LES NUBIANS
The Album
STORES NO
LES

Si l'auteur commence la poésie pour lui-même, c'est
pour d'autres qu'il la termine et la publie. Choisir,
dans un domaine déterminé, tout ce qui lui paraît
digne et capable de provoquer chez le lecteur un
choc de beauté, voilà l'objet de son effort.
C'est dire aussi qu'il prétend trouver un ECHO et
que le lecteur inconnu ratifiera son choix.
-Jacques Chevrier

Writers may start a poem for themselves, but they
finish and publish it for other people. Their
efforts are focused on choosing whatever they feel is
appropriate and capable of evoking a beauty shock,
in a particular field. In other words, they may also
claim to find an ECHO and the unknown reader
validates their choice.

-Jacques Chevrier

☥
— · —
Motherland

La Terre-Mère
— · —
☥

Reste que faire remonter au jour une
identité fracturée est autre chose que
de se souvenir d'un passé trop lourd
de douleur ou d'apprendre dans
les livres ce qu'il fut.

Seuls les mots de l'imaginaire, les
poèmes, et les chants peuvent rendre
présents ce qui à jamais échappe. Le
travail de l'art est ici déterminant.

✝×✝✗×✝×✝×✝×✗×✝ ✝✗×✝✗×✝✗××✝×✝ ✝×✗✝×✗×✝×✝×✝

"Bringing to light a fractured identity
is not the same as remembering a
pain-filled past or learning what it
actually was from books.

"Only imaginary words, poems, and
songs can let surface what has escaped.
Art plays a determinant role here."

-Jacques Audinet

ELLE EST NÉE EN NUBIE

On dit que pour le collectionneur, le temps se déguise en artiste.

They say the collector views time as an artist in disguise.

Souleymane Diamanka

A long voyage begins with just one step. Mauritania proverb.

Un long voyage commence d'un seul pas. Nouakchott 2004.

Elle Est Née En Nubie

Le jour où la princesse s'est assise sur le Nil
Le soleil souriait de tous ses feux dans le ciel nu
Pendant que les courants la guidaient jusqu'à l'île
Le vent chantait des airs paisibles de bienvenue
Elle, les yeux dans le quotidien de ses ancêtres
Comme devant le tableau d'un paysage vivant
Qui venait s'écrire sur sa mémoire comme une lettre
Elle apprenait par coeur ce bout du monde d'antan
Le jour où la princesse s'est couchée sur le Nil
La lune a veillé et la nuit n'est pas tombée
Elle est belle comme le chant des femmes qui broient le mil
Quand par un doux chagrin son oeil est inondé
Elle m'a ramené un peu de terre de là-bas
Ce sable dur qui porte la même couleur que sa peau
Dans sa poitrine bat le coeur d'une reine de Saba
Et un scarabée orne sa nuque comme un joyau.

Souleymane Diamanka

She Was Born In Nubia

The day the princess sat on the Nile
The sun smiled its brightest in the naked sky
While the currents guided her to the isle
The wind sang peaceful tunes of welcome
She gazed at the scene of her ancestors
Like she was studying a live landscape painting
Which was inscribed in her mind like a letter
She learned a part of this long-ago world by heart
The day the princess lay on the Nile
The sun watched and night did not fall
She's as lovely as the song of women grinding grain
When her eyes are streamed with sweet sorrow
She brought me back some soil from back there
This hard sand was the same color as her skin
In her chest the heart of a Queen of Sheba beats
And a scarab adorns her neck like a jewel.

- Souleymane Diamanka

HEAVEN

L'écriture exprime les convulsions de la vie intime qui ne s'apaise
que dans l'harmonie retrouvée, dans l'accord originel
qui scelle la réconciliation de l'homme avec le cosmos.

×××+ ⁺×××××⁺×⁺ ⁺×××⁺×××××⁺×⁺

Writing expresses the convulsions of private lives that
    only subside with rediscovered harmony, with the original accord
        that seals humankind's reconciliation with the cosmos.

-Jacques Chevrier

Le Paradis

Le paradis
Est dans ma tête
Je l'assemble
Le construit
Comme les enfers où j'ai vécu
Au-delà des souhaits, des prières, des
idées
Au-delà de la voix, du mouvement,
des larmes
Au-delà du désir,...l'énergie et de
l'analyse
Qui ont autant de masse critique que
Du muscle, de l'os, du sang.

Fixe mon attention
Sur mon intention
J'en prends l'entière responsabilité
Reconnais quand j'imprègne mon
propre paradis
D'idées qui drainent ma force
Comme la conspiration qui use
d'invisibles ficelles
Pour me mouvoir dans le
Royaume de ma propre inconsistance.

Si je peux juste
Nier cela
La haine – On n'veut pas des gens de
ton espèce ici
Le blâme – C'est pas d'ma faute
L'orgueil – J'sais pas d'quoi tu m'parles
La peur – J'peux pas, j'peux pas le faire
J'exaucerai la prophétie

Peut-être jamais tu ne sauras
Où mènent mes empreintes
Quand je serai partie
Peut-être jamais tu ne verras
Le chemin que j'ai choisi
Tu ne verras peut-être jamais scintiller
mon étoile
Ni mes constellations se mouvoir

Mais je peux le rêver
Je peux l'être
Cette lune
Ce nuage
Ce ciel
Je peux être
Sauvé
Comblé
Heureux
Réel

Ne me dit pas
Que le paradis est scellé
Aux goûts
D'autres plus sains que moi
J'ai moi-même plein de failles

Je refuse de perdre mon esprit
Dans un chagrin emprisonné dans
L'illusion de ma finitude

Tu ne peux ni me dire
Ni me faire descendre de mon nuage
Là n'est pas ta place
Mon nuage m'appartient

N'essaye même pas
De décider pour moi
De la couleur de mon âme
Du métal de mon dessein
De la texture de mon esprit
Ce n'est pas ta place
Mon esprit m'appartient
J'appartiens à
Mon esprit a droit de vie pour
Explorer mon propre
Territoire délivré
J'assemble mon paradis ensemble
Je rêve mon paradis ensemble
J'aime mon paradis ensemble
Je souhaite mon paradis ensemble
Je choisis mon paradis ensemble
Je chante mon paradis ensemble
Je connais mon paradis
Je connais mon paradis

Tout en me déplaçant
Où, quand, comment
Je vis
Ici, là-bas
Après, maintenant, bientôt
Je serai
Ouaaaaaouh !!!
Tous ensemble à nouveau
Nous saurons
Qui, quoi, où, quand
Comment, pourquoi
Je suis, tu es
Une créature du Paradis.

Heaven

Heaven
is in my mind
I put it together
construct it
like the hells in which I've lived
out of wishes, prayers, ideas
out of voice, motion, tears
out of desire, energy and analysis
which have as much critical mass as
muscle, bone, blood

focus my attention
on my intention
take full responsibility
recognize when I preemt my own
heaven
with ideas that drain my power
like the conspiracy that uses invisible
strings to
keep me moving in the
realm of my own inconsistency

if I can just
deny that
hate blame pride fear
self fulfilling prophecy

you may never know
where my footprints lead
after I am gone away
you may never see
the path I choose
may never see the twinkling of my star
see my constellations move

but I can dream it
I can be it
that moon
that cloud
that sun
that sky
I can be
that safe
that full
that happy
that real

don't tell me
heaven's sealed
for the likes of those
holier than me
I've got plenty holes of my own

I refuse to
lose my mind
to the sadness locked in the
illusion of my finitude

you can't make me
tell me come down off my clouds
that is not your place
my clouds belong to me

don't you dare presume to
decide for me the
color of my soul
the metal of my intention
the element of my spirit

that is not your place
my spirit belongs to me
I belong to
my spirit has the birthright to
explore my own
uncharted territory
I put my heaven together
I dream my heaven together
I love my heaven together
I wish my heaven together
I choose my heaven together
I poet my heaven together
I know my heaven
I know my heaven

as I make/shift me
where, how, when
I live
here, there
then, now, soon
I will be
whaaaaaaaaaaaa!!!!!
all back together again
knowing
who/what/where/when
how/why
I am
you are
a heavenly being

Chuma

Fisiwe Zwana

LES ENTRAILLES DU MONDE

They say that there are knots in blood
ties that can never come loose.

Intermixing exposes, displays, makes visible,
points out, like an artist's model, like an image in
the foreground, like a prototype, what our soci-
eties carry, where they are heading and how. In
short, it signifies where humanity is heading.

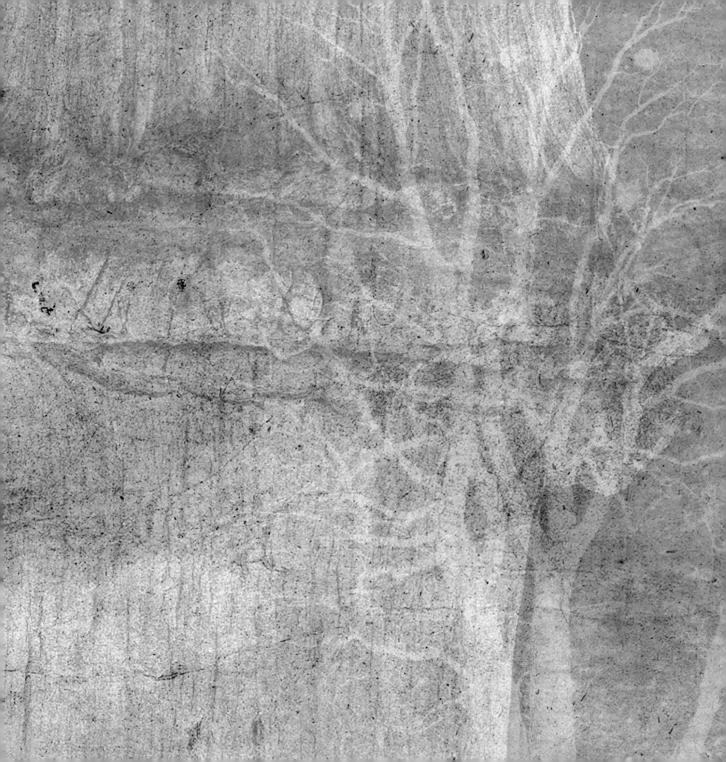

Les Entrailles du Monde

Terre d'origine,
Moi, femme
Sur mes continents
L'homme voyage et avec lui ses lan-
gages
Combien de poèmes
Sont nés de nos baisers
Aux langues entre-mêlées
Combien de métissages ...Métisses...
Sages...
Sont l'héritage
De nos corps chevauchés
Au rythme de mes désirs...plaisirs

Veux-tu connaître la géographie de
mon corps
Pour un nouveau corps à corps
Ne vois-tu pas le mont Cameroun
vibrer
Devant cette nudité s'offre à toi
l'humanité

Moi qui te lie par trois fois à la vie
Regarde-moi telle que je suis

Quant à moi je revendique

Ma féminité par mon mental
Dans ce monde infernal
Oh j'ai mal, j'ai le mal de la bêtise
humaine.
Je suis une lady issue d'un royaume
Où les princes et les rois ne sont que
des fantômes

Moi, femme
Gardienne de mémoire
Mère..... d'espoirs
Pilier entre les hommmes
Et les divinités
Ma spiritualité est enracinée
Dans la vérité, la réalité

Reine de coeur pas de chirurgie sur
mon facial
Rien que de l'esthétisme dans mon
style
Les types de modèles
Pour mon type, je suis le modèle
Au top comme elle, mieux qu'elle
Les vagues de modèles en vogue se
démodent
Car je suis le mode de femme qui ne

respecte pas les codes

Moi, femme
Moi, femme
Moi, femme
mon ventre porte l'humanité
De mon sein coule l'éternité

Je mets au monde l'univers
.... L'universalité
Moi, femme
combattante sur tous les fronts pour
défendre le nom
Du fruit de mes entrailles

Mille fois séparé
Mille fois retrouvé
Mille fois mort
Mille fois resucité
En moi
Femme
Je défie l'espace et le temps

Moi qui te lie par trois fois
À la vie
Regarde-moi telle que je suis

Anouch

Zuga

The Womb of the World

Original land
I, woman
On my continents
Man travels and brings
along his language
How many poems
Were born from our kisses
with intermingled tongues
How many mixed race children
Sound children
Are the heritage
Of our bodies intertangled
To the rhythm of my desires
Pleasures

Want to know the geography
of my body
In a new embrace
Don't you see Mount Cameroon
vibrate?
Facing this nudity, to you is
offered humanity

I who link you three times to life
Look at me the way I am

As for me, I claim
My femininity through
my mental state
In this infernal world
I hurt, I hurt from human stupidity
I'm a lady descended from a kingdom
Where the princes and kings are
just shadows

I, guardian of memories
Mother of hope
Pillar between humans
and divinities
My spirituality is rooted in truth
and reality

Queen of hearts, no surgery
on my face
Nothing but aesthetics in my style
The types of models
For my type, I'm the model
At the top like her, better than her
The waves of models go in and
out of fashion
Since I am the kind of woman who
doesn't respect the codes

I, woman
My belly holds humanity
From my breast flows eternity
I give birth to the Universe
Universality

I, woman
Fighter
On all fronts
To defend the name
Of the fruit of my womb

A thousand times separated
A thousand times recovered
A thousand times dead
A thousand times resuscitated
In me
Woman
I defy space and time

I who link you three times to life
Look at me
Look at me the way I am.

- Anouch Adjarian and Zuga

Au Pied De L'histoire De Mon Peuple

Raconte - moi
La parole du griot
Qui chante l'Afrique
Des temps immémoriaux
il dit
ces rois patients
sur les cîmes du silence
et la beauté des vieux
aux sourires fânés
Mon passé revenu
Du fond de ma mémoire
Comme un serpent totem
à mes chevilles lié
Ma solitude
Et mes espoirs brisés
Qu'apporterais-je
à mes enfants
Si j'ai perdu leur âme ?

-Véronique Tadjo

Tell me the words of the griot
Who sings of Africa
From time immemorial
He speaks of
These pataient kings
On the summits of silence
and the beauty of the elders
with faded smiles
My past returns
From the depths of my memory
Like a snake totem
At my ankles tied
to my solitude
and my dashed hopes
What shall I offer
My children
If I have lost my soul?

On dit que les chapitres de l'histoire du peuple noir
ont été effacés avec le sang de ses ancêtres.

They say that chapters in the history of black people
were erased with the blood of their ancestors.

-SD

Au pied de l'histoire de mon peuple

Un matin, je me suis assis
Au pied de l'histoire de mon peuple
J'ai posé mes questions lourdes de sang
A même le sol
Et j'ai pleuré dans ma langue natale
Quand j'ai entendu
L' Echo

Souleymane Diamanka

At the foot of the history of my people

One morning I sat down
At the foot of the history of my people
I set my blood-laden questions on the bare ground
And I wept in my native tongue
When I heard
The Echo

- Souleymane Diamanka

SOLIDE

✝×✝

On dit que le fou du roi se fout du roi et que le roi rit.

✝×

They say that the court jester mocks the king and the king laughs.

-SD

On dit que la balance de la justice penche du côté de ceux qui pèsent.

✝×

They say that the scales of justice lean towards those who carry weight.

-SD

Solide

Raconte ma soeur ton histoire
Mon histoire commence quelque part
en plein cauchemar
C'est le ventre vide que je marche,
pieds nus
J'entends les bombes et je presse le pas
C'est le souffle de la vie qui me porte
là-bas

Et je cours...
Il faut survivre

Reste Solide
Et ne pas l'oublier
Même si le monde est perfide
Joue-le encore
Lance les dés
Reste lucide
What goes down shall come up

Quel est ma soeur ton regard ?
Triste quand j'y pense
Des montagnes de béton
Ma prison immense
Je respire par procuration – sous
perfusion -
Suis-je l'enfant damné de la nation ?

Et tout brille dans la ville
Mais pas dans le coeur des gens
Des diplômes plein les poches, pas
d'embauche
C'est moche
Il n'y a pas de place pour moi ici

Et je cours...
(Ne pas oublier)
je cours
(Dans la ville)
Stay Strong

Reste Solide
What goes up must come down...

C'est le vent qui souffle
Qui m'amène là-bas, qui m'appelle
là-bas
Un nouveau son de vie
C'est mon coeur qui bat

Celia – Les Nubians

Helene – Les Nubians

Solid

Tell your tale, my sister
My tale begins in a cautionary bad
dream
Belly empty and bare feet I walk
I hear the bombs I speed up my walk
It's the Breath of Life that is leading
me there

And I run
Need to survive

Stay Solid
and Never forget
Even if the world is grinding
Roll the dice again
Play to win
Keep it Savvy
What goes down shall come up

Sister, what's in your sight?

Sadness within my eyes
Mountains of concrete
My prison is gigantic
I breathe under assistance
On a drip
I'm the Damned Child of this
nation?

'Cause everything shines uptown
But not in people's heart
Heads full of skills and degrees
Unemployed
It sucks
There's no place for me in here

And I run...
(Never forget)
And I run
(In the city)
Stay strong

Stay Solid
and Never forget
Even if the world is grinding
Roll the dice again
Play to win
Keep it savvy
What goes up must come down

The Wind is blowing
Calling me over there
Flying me over there

Yet I can hear. A new sound of Life
My heartbeat

- Les Nubians

37

Memory frees the future.

La mémoire libère le futur.

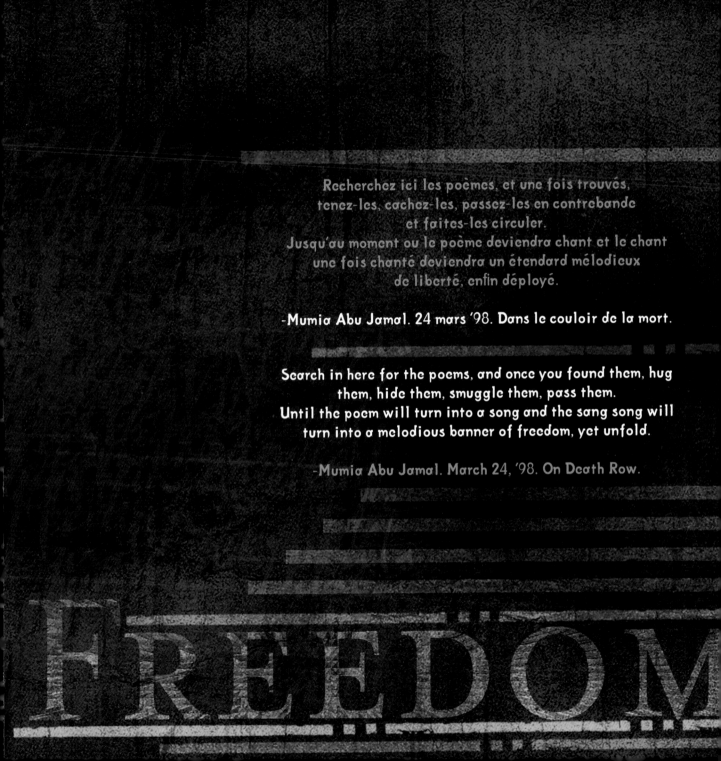

Recherchez ici les poèmes, et une fois trouvés,
tenez-les, cachez-les, passez-les en contrebande
et faites-les circuler.
Jusqu'au moment ou le poème deviendra chant et le chant
une fois chanté deviendra un étendard mélodieux
de liberté, enfin déployé.

-Mumia Abu Jamal. 24 mars '98. Dans le couloir de la mort.

Search in here for the poems, and once you found them, hug
them, hide them, smuggle them, pass them.
Until the poem will turn into a song and the sang song will
turn into a melodious banner of freedom, yet unfold.

-Mumia Abu Jamal. March 24, '98. On Death Row.

FREEDOM

Liberté

LIBERTÉ, LIBERTÉ, LIBERTÉ
Elle vient et je veux rentrer avec elle, maintenant
LIBERTÉ
TOUTE PUISSANTE
Et avant d'être esclave
De cette scène hip hop
Je rentre chez moi et j'balance des rimes libres
LIBERTÉ TOUTE PUISSANTE, LIBERTÉ VIENS À MOI
C'est vrai, j'avoue
J'étais la seule à porter l'esclavage comme de vieilles sapes pendant plus de 300 ans
D'ailleurs, mon âme gagne le prix d'élégance
Tu vois, j'suis tellement puissante et Funky fresh
Que mes flatulences sonnent comme un biiiiiiiiiiiiiiiiiiiiiiip !
Car toute cette merde n'est qu'un test
Oui, toute cette merde n'est qu'un test
Et je suis la Reine D-E-E-S-S-E *
La Déesse entra dans la place pour mettre un terme au racket
Elle vit un démon au MIC , dégaina la magie noire du verbe

Le show, elle l'avait maté
Mais merde il pouvait pas comprendre
Ses rimes venaient d'une autre planète
Respect exigé
Même s'ils l'appelèrent le bandit des mots
Parce que comme une voleuse elle s'était emparée du show
Déesse des 7 mers , elle avait l'truc qui coulait dans son flow
Elle donnait vie à chaque souffle à de nouveaux MCs
Qui faisaient offrande de leurs rimes pour transformer des putes du MIC en lyricistes
Elle avait tant aimé le monde, qu'elle révélait aux enragés leur propre esprit
Des poèmes d'une éternelle pureté ; et les vrais MCs furent bénis
Des MCs défièrent les lyrics de la Terre
Mais Yo, cette déesse les a balayés d'un simple et uni-vers
Elle donna 24 heures à la Terre, pour se préparer à la guerre
Mais Yo, cette déesse était si salement inspirée
Que son flow, même une pluie de

météores n'aurait pu le laver
Bien sûr, elle savait
Que ses mots meurtrissaient

Alors l'Impératrice du Verbe
Quitta la Terre et sur Mars alla régner
Comme Farrakhan elle fit marcher
Un million d'anges à ses côtés
Comme un Sonny Carson sidéral
A des bandes de martiens elle délivra la morale
Comme Moïse elle partagea
Les flows sur la planète
Et la colère s'empara de Yemoja*

Merde !
C'était terrifiant
Son style frappait comme la foudre

Tous les MCs l'appelèrent Titan
Car elle était bien plus que
« notorious* » par les flows qu'elle crachait
Bouddha se leva et la défia
Mais c'est assis qu'il se retrouva
En position du lotus
Il avait oublié qu'elle était en mission
Jamais plus il ne se lèvera sans sa

Queen GodIs

permission
Déesse
Du Soleil, de la Lune et des étoiles du
ghetto
Puisque Vénus versifiait pour les
femmes
Elle quitta Mars en laissant pendre les
micros
Pour la « Res-Erection » des âmes
Par le va-et-vient de son flow
Simplement parce que GodIs était une
femme qui s'la racontait, les martiens
voulurent squatter le MIC
C'était peine perdue car avant de partir
Elle les avait inondés de rimes si
meurtrières
Qu'en voulant les traverser ils
coulèrent
Il y avait un dieu nommé hip hop
Qui vivait sur la planète Vénus
Il voulut lui aussi vaincre GodIs
Jusqu'à ce qu'elle freestyle avec son
pénis
J't'assure
Parce que Yo, moi-même je l'ai vue
Elle arracha le MIC telle MC Bobbitt,
et le planta sur ses étagères

Godis femme noire
Son style venu d'ailleurs
Elle envoya Lucifer au diable parce
qu'il la trouvait trop mortelle
Je suis la Reine Déesse

De mon sein coulent des rythmes
lactés qui nourrissent les mots nou-
veaux-nés
Tranquille je
Suis bénie
Oui je
Suis la Reine Mère
La Parole Sagesse est ma fille
La Parole de Vie est son frère
Ma progéniture deviendra verbe
Mes menstruations n'auraient pas pu
la tuer
Mes laxatifs poétiques
Régulent votre esprit
Le cordon du micro est ombilical
Quand je perd mes eaux mentales
Mon flow devient spirituel et « lyrical »
Le Mot est né

Ils croyaient qu'en menottant mon
esprit, en coupant ma langue je ne
pourrais plus

Crier pour être libre
Mais j'ai ouvert mon esprit, et par
télépathie j'ai crié pour ma liberté :

LIBERTÉ, LIBERTÉ, LIBERTÉ
Elle vient et je veux rentrer avec elle,
maintenant
LIBERTÉ
TOUTE PUISSANTE
Et avant d'être esclave
De cette scène hip hop
Je rentre chez moi et j'balance des
rimes libres
LIBERTÉ TOUTE PUISSANTE,
LIBERTÉ VIENS A MOI...

* Déesse de la mer. Brésil
*« G-O-D-I-S » GodIs angl=Déesse
* Notorious Big a.k.a Christopher
Wallace, rappeur

- Queen GodIs

Freedom

FREEDOM!…

Coming and I want to go home now!

FREEDOM!…

Over me

And before I be a slave
To this hip hop game
I'll go home to my room and
kick a free
Freedom over me

Yes, I must confess
I've rocked slavery like a hand-me-
down for over three hundred years
And still my soul wins best dressed
I mean I am so fly and funky fresh
My flatulations sound like
BEEEEEP!…
'cause all this Sh… is just a test
Yes, all this Sh… is just a test

But I am the Queen G-O-D-I-S

The GodIs stepped into the room to
put an end to all racket
Saw a demon on the mic, pulled out
her lyrical black magic
The show, she ran it
But suckas could not understand it
As if her rhymes came from
another planet
Respect demanded
Even though they called her lyrical
bandit
'Cause like a thief she stole the show
GodIs of the seven seas, had suckas
drowning in her flows
Gave life to new MCs when she
exhaled out her nose…
Sacrificed their rhymes to make lyri-
cists out of mic hos

For she so loved the world, she gave
biters their own spirits
And all the REAL MCs got blessed
with eternal lyrics
MCs tried to battle with lyrics from
the earth,
But this GodIs took them out with a

single uni-Verse
She told the Earth to rehearse and
gave her twenty-four hours.
This GodIs was so nasty, not even
meteor showers could make her flows
clean
She was so keen to the fact that
Her lyrics left scars
And so this lyrical tzar
Left the earth to rule Mars
Like Farrakhan she was starting
With a million angels marching
Like an alien Sonny Carson
She lectured gangs made of Martians
Like Moses she was parting
Flows on the planet
Yemoja couldn't stand it
Damn it!
It was frightening
Her whole style was like lightning
And instead of calling her "Biggie"
All the MCs called her Titan
'Cause she was more than Notorious
for the flows that she was spitting
Buddha stood up and tried to battle,
But He ended up just sitting

Queen GodIs

In a lotus position
He forgot that she was on a mission
He won't be getting up until he asks
for her permission
GODIS
Of the Sun
Of the Moon
and of the ghetto super-Stars
And like Venus who rhymed
for women,
She left mics dangling on Mars
"Res-Erecting" souls
Leaving flows coming and coming
The Martians tried to hog the mic just
'cause GodIs was a woman
Fronting!
But that's alright though 'cause before
she left the planet
She was spitting flows so deep,
The Martians sank just 'cause they
swam it
There was a god called hip hop
Who lived on the planet Venus
He tried to battle GodIs
'Til she free-styled with his penis
I mean this,

'Cause I saw it for myself
She ripped the mic like MC Bobbitt
and stuck it on her shelf.

Black Woman GodIs
They deemed her whole style exotic
She sent Lucifer to hell just 'cause he
thought he was the hottest

Queen G-O-D-I-S
I nurture newborn lyrics with lactics
rythms in my breast
No stress I
Yes I
Bless I
Am the Queen Mother
Word of Wisdom is my daughter
Word of Life is her brother
I raise these seeds to be lyrics
Menstruation couldn't kill it
My poetic laxatives
Yes, they regulate your spirit
The microphone cord is umbilical
When my mental waters break
My flows be lyrical and spiritual
WORD IS BORN…

They thought that if they handcuffed
my spirit and shackled my tongue that
I couldn't scream to be free!,
But I just opened up my mind and
screamed for freedom telepathically…

FREEDOM!

Coming and I want to go home now!

FREEDOM!

Over me

And before I be a slave…
To this hip hop game,
I'll go home to my room
And kick a free

Freedom over me,/ Freedom over me!,
Freedom over we!!

- Queen GodIs

43

La Ville

×

Urban city Life

Mais la ville est une menace. Quand elle n'est pas pétrie d'une vieille mémoire, soigneusement amplifiée, sa logique est inhumaine. Le désert y naît sous la jolie mécanique des néons et des dictatures automobiles (...) Il faut désormais (...) réamorcer d'autres tracés, en sorte de susciter en ville, une contre-ville. Et autour de la ville, réinventer la campagne. L' architecte, c'est pourquoi, doit se faire musicien, sculpteur, peintre, et l'urbaniste, poète.

Patrick Chamoiseau

But the city is danger. When it is not kneaded like an old memory, carefully amplified, her logic is inhuman. A desert is born there beneath the mechanical joy of neon and the reign of automobiles... The urban planner must from now... on restart new trails in order to arouse a countercity in the city. And around the city reinvent the countryside. That's why the architect must become a musician, sculptor, painter... and the urban planner a poet.

Patrick Chamoiseau

I watch my century rushing by, in its last moments, numbed by the creaking cold, in the steely, concrete night. The flashes of silver blades on the car exteriors, the store windows, shine like artificial, vanishing stars, the ones in the sky are veiled by dirt and pollution. And in this moment of the end of time, even though the cold numbs my fingers, I wonder.
LN. 12:25 a.m.

Je regarde mon siècle courir, dans ses derniers instants engourdis par le froid qui grince, dans une nuit métallique et bétonnée. Les éclats d'argent lamé sur les carrosseries des voitures, les vitrines, brillent comme des étoiles artificielles et disparues, celles du ciel voilé par la crasse la pollution. Et dans cet instant de fin du temps, je m'inspire, même si le froid engourdit mes doigts. Je m'interroge.

LN. Steel night in Paris

Un pays sans clôture est un pays sans ennemi.

Those who have no fence around their land have no enemies.

-Proverbe Burundi

WAR IN BABYLON

The Lord is my rock and my fortress
and my deliverer, my God my strength,
in whom I will trust: my shield and the
loom of my salvation, my shoulder.

-Psalms 18 vs. 2.

War in Babylon

Babylone est mourante et la voix de Dieu
Appelle son messager : « AIDE-LES »
Mais cet appel tombe dans les oreilles
agacées d'un messager indisposé...
« Seigneur, je ne veux pas les aider »
« Ils sont mauvais et je les verrai mourir
comme ils ont regardé mourir
Sous leurs yeux tant de fois qu'on ne peut
les énumérer
Et Dieu appelle :   « SAUVE-LES »
Et le messager de Dieu répond :
Je sais que ce n'est pas ma volonté mais ta
volonté qui doit être accomplie
Mais je ne veux pas les sauver...
Mais essayer d'échapper à ta volonté est
comme tenter de fuir le soleil
Ou essayer de passer entre les gouttes du
déluge en espérant ne pas être mouillé
Seigneur, ta gloire c'est ta pitié et l'amour
que tu verses goutte à goutte

Pour ceux même qui n'en sont pas dignes
...Comme moi...Et c'est ce qui te fait Dieu
Je suis simplement et seulement un
humain
Qui éprouve une grande gêne à aider ceux
qui m'ont blessé
Babylone est trop mauvaise pour être
sauvée
Son empire a dévoré la terre et enfanté des
nations
Bâties sur les fondations de Sodome et
Gommore, Nineveh et Rome
Babylone n'est pas ma patrie
Et je demande à Dieu que vous m'envoyiez
ailleurs
Y'a-t-il autre chose que je peux faire pour
vous
Plutôt que de nouer le dialogue avec ceux
qui vendraient le Porc de votre temple
Les habitants de Gog et Magog avec leurs

habitudes de chien
Et une fois encore la voix de Dieu appelle :
« SAUVE-LES »
Mais Seigneur, s'il vous plaît, ne pourrais-
je pas être fait gardien du feu de l'enfer
Pour m'assurer qu'il est assez brûlant pour
ceux qui semble-t-il n'en ont jamais assez
Ne pourrais-je pas attiser les flammes qui
les consument
Pour augmenter leur punition et leur
tourment
C'est un hurlement que je vous adresse car
du plus profond de mes poumons
Je travaille à la compassion
Mais que c'est dur d'aimer ceux si préoc-
cupés par la vanité et la mode
Ils prisent seulement les plaisirs terrestres
Et c'est au-dessus de mes pauvres forces de
les aimer

Jamarhl Crawford

War in Babylon

War inna' de' Babylon, war inna' de' Babylon, war inna' de' Babylon
Babylon De-eeeaaa-ad

Babylon is dying and the voice of God
call to his messenger: "Help them" but this
call falls on the reluctant
ears of an unwilling messenger...
"Lord, I do not want to help them"
"They are wicked and I will watch them die
as they have witnessed death at their hands
on occasions too numerous to name."
God calls: "Save them"
and the messenger of God replies
"I know that it is not my will but your will
to be done,
but I don't want to save them...
but trying to escape your will is like attempting
to run from the sun

or trying to dodge raindrops during the
Great Flood
attempting not to get wet.
Lord your glory is your mercy & love
which are
doled out even to those who do not deserve
it,
Like me and this is what makes you God.
I am merely & simply human
Finding great discomfort in helping those
who have hurt me
Babylon is too wicked to save
Her empire has swallowed the earth
and gave birth to nations
built on the foundations of Sodom &
Gomorrah, Nineveh
and Rome
Babylon is not my home
and I ask Lord that you send me elsewhere
is there nothing else I can do to help you

rather than enter in to dialogue
with those who would sell hog from your
synagogue
the inhabitants of Gog & Magog
with the habits of a dog...
and God's voice once again said "Help
them"
"but Lord, please can't I be made steward
of the hell fire
making sure it is hot enough,
for those who seemingly never got enough?
Couldn't I fan the flames that consume
them
and for their added punishment & torment
yell "I told you so" at the top of my lungs
I am working on compassion
but it is hard to love those so concerned
with vanity & fashion
they treasure only worldly pleasure
and it is beyond my power to love them.

- Jamarhl Crawford

49

But the city is danger. When it is not kneaded like an old memory, carefully amplified, her logic is inhuman. A desert is born there beneath the mechanical joy of neon and the reign of automobiles. The urban planner must from now on restart new trails in order to arouse a counter city in the city. And around the countryside. That's why the architect become a musician, sculptor, painter and planner a poet.

Patrick Chan

PROSE ELECTRIQUE PART 1

Nous devons être les poètes de notre vie, et d'abord dans les plus petites choses.
We must be the poets of our life, and in the smallest things initially.
-Friedrich Nietzsche

On dit qu'à force de regarder dans leur dos, les gens marchent à reculons dans la rue.
They say if people keep looking over their shoulders, they'll end up walking backwards in the street.
-SD

ProsE ÉlEctriquE – Part 1

J'ai volé l'ombre d'une passante,
j'ai choisi...
Une silhouette parmi des simulacres...
Une nébuleuse, une flamme parmi les
femmes, brûlure solaire imprimée au mouvement du sol comme le battement régulier de
mes lignes inégalées
J'te vois venir,
j'entends tes pas,
J'suis pas vraiment moi et t'es quelqu'un
d'autre...
Mais lequel...(lequel) est l'ombre (est
l'ombre)...de qui (de qui) ?
Tu voulais dévaler les notes de mon imagination, circuler dans mon souffle, ressentir les
pulsations d'un cœur qui n'est pas
l'tien ...Comme... un interrogatoire qui m'
lâche pas tant qu' j'ai pas craché l'morceau .
Mais j' sais qu' si tu m'entends J'entends tu m'
vois...et toi
Ca m' gêne, moi j' t' imagines seulement sub-
liminale poursuite du frisson qui parcours

mon corps branché sur la prose électrique...
Libre est qui déséquilibre l'ombre qui le suit,
la sème ou la somme de cesser sa somnolence
horizontale...
Les ombres qu'on tient à part s'appartiennent
toutes... la nuit !

Si Je suis moi, tu es mon reflet ,alors elle ...
est ma troisième personne ?...
Personne répond.
Les bouches d'égouts savent par où tu
respires esquisse secrète , décalcomanie en
dédale, danseuse articulée le long de l'envers
du décor
Je serais né avec elle sans lui avoir soufflé
mot ? ? ?
La somnambule épie mes pas, s'arrête... ça
va ?...

Une brise dans les branches, une éclair-
cie souligne son sein... Elle a glissé sous
ma porte, cette enveloppe sans destin que

j'appelle l'être anonyme à laquelle il manque
tout un alphabet...
Folle et solitaire, elle titube à l'agonie en
cherchant son remède existentiel au bout des
nuits.

J'ai ...trébuché...
Maintenant mon pas résonne
derrière le sien , ma traînée absurde et
sourde vacille au chant des lampadaires. Plus
d'heure sous le ciel de la lampe et le soleil du
plafond
Jette ton malheur sur le tapis , j' le couvrirai
d'un drap !

Diluée dans la nuit , dissipée elle disparaît
aux yeux du pauvre spectateur du spectre en
soustraction avançant imbibé pour envier ton
imperméabilité maladive.

Rêve d'une autre rive.

John Banzaï

ElEctric ProsE – Part 1

I stole the shadow of a passerby
I chose...
A silhouette among pretenders...
A nebula, a flame among women, solar burn
stamped along the ground like the regular
beat of my uneven lines.
I see you coming
I hear your footsteps.
I'm not really me, and you're somebody else...
But who... "who?" is the shadow..."the
shadow"of who? "of who?"
You wanted to rush down the notes of my
imagination, circulate inside my breath, feel
the beating of a heart which isn't yours...
like...an interrogation that won't leave me
until I spit some answer out.
But I know that if you hear me "I hear you,"
you see me, "what about you?"
That bothers me, I only imagine you, sub-
liminal pursuit of the thrill travelling over
my body hooked up to my "prose électrique."

Free is the one who unbalances the shadow
that follows him, shakes her off or orders her
to cease hers horizontal somnolence...
Shadows we keep apart belong together in
the dark.

If I am me, you are my reflection, then is
SHE my third person?
Nobody answers.
The manholes know the place where you
breathe, secret sketch, decal in a maze,
dancer articulated on the other side of the
picture.
Was I born with her, without breathing a
word to her???
The sleepwalker watches my steps closely,
stops: "How is it going?"
A breeze in the branches, a sunny spell
underlines her breast. She slipped under
my door this no destiny message, called
anonymous let-her, which is missing a whole

alphabet...
Wild and lonely, she staggers agonizingly
searching for an existential remedy till the
end of nights.
I...stumbled... "Whoops!"
Now my footstep echoes
behind hers, my deaf and dull trail vacillate
to the chant of the streetlamps
Timeless...under the lamp sky and the ceiling
sun...
Throw your misfortune on the floor, I'll cover
it with a sheet.
Diluted in the night, dissipated she disappears from the poor spectator's eyes of the
subtracted spectrum, walking soaking drunk
to envy her sickly impermeability.

Dream of another shore.

- John Banzaï

Que tu l'attendes ou non,
demain viendra.
-Proverbe Liberia

DEMAIN LIVE

If you wait for tomorrow,
tomorrow comes. If you
don't wait for tomorrow,
tomorrow comes.
-Liberia Proverb

NYC

New York ! Je dis New York,
laisse affluer le sang noir dans
ton sang
Qu'il dérouille tes articulations
d'acier, comme une huile de vie
Qu'il donne
à tes ponts
la courbe des
croupes et la
souplesse des
lianes.
Voici revenir
les temps très
anciens, l'unité
retrouvée la
réconciliation
du Lion, du
Taureau et de
l'Arbre
L'idée liée à
l'acte l'oreille
au cœur le
signe au sens.

New York, I say New
York, let the black blood
flow into your blood, may
it remove the rust from
your steel joints, like an
oil of life
May it give your bridges
the curve of hips and the
suppleness of vines...
Here comes the ancient
times, where unity
lies, the reconciliation
of the lion, the bull, and
the tree
The idea linked to
action, the ear linked to
the heart and the sign to
the meaning. -Leopold Sedar Senghor

NYC

J'ai affronté les obstacles grâce à la chanson
Enfants des berceuses courant autour du maïs
Sans mères pour veiller à leur maturité future
La rage silencieuse des pères peut s'amplifier pendant des jours au-delà des murs
De la prison de Sing Sing
Où les accusations arbitraires côtoient des paroissiens coupables.

On se plaint de ne pas avoir de héros dans le coin
Des immigrés débarquent de l'avion et embrassent le sol en entendant injures, poèmes d'amour et propositions indécentes
Deviendrai-je millionnaire ?
Les feuilles tombent des épines, l'artiste esquisse des personnages sans langues
Transmettant de faux messages sur ...
Pourquoi est-ce que ta main fait le signe de croix sur ma figure ?

On crée des boissons édulcorées pour adoucir la peine
Je n'avais pas écouté Dieu lorsqu'elle disait « fais plus attention à moi »
Alors mes filles sont devenues à moitié sourdes

Je salsa, merengue et mambo ma ballade quotidienne à travers la ville
Mes oreilles saignent du défaitisme des autres
Si on me demande où est passé l'amour, il est parti quand j'étais petite ;
Je jouais au-dessus des douilles de crack
Sautais à la corde entre des bouteilles d'alcool
Faisait la course sur des cadavres.
Mes désirs se balancent comme le sommet

des arbres avec l'espoir de m'évader et de m'élever vers la réussite

Le béton est devenu le masque que je porte
Je cherche le juste espace pour m'étendre
Tandis que je mendie une pièce ou deux pour racheter ma lucidité,
Pétales de fleur assis dans un verre au sommet de ma créativité.
ON accélère jusqu'à la page où l'on veut être
Nos livres de biologie datent de 1910
Vivant dans le passé,
Nous intégrons,
Léchons des culs
Décrochons des diplômes

Tout cela au nom de la survie
Vivant de jour de paye en jour de paie!
Est-ce tout ce que m'offre la vie à New York City
La vie à New York City

Glorifiez Brooklyn disent-ils
Allez à Central Park
Faites-vous agresser et violer
Courez, transpirez votre désespoir
Inhalant pollution et brume chaque jour

Alors qu'on me dit de ne faire qu'un avec la nature dans une cage appelée parc
Mes instincts m'abandonnent dans l'obscurité
Une séance à 9$50, du pop-corn rassi et j'me fait tout un film
Des rats à longue queue réchauffent mes pieds

Où vais-je aller pour éviter la déchirure,
Même les amoureux se disputent dès le début pour une facture.
C'est encore Dupont qui a eu l'augmentation aujourd'hui.
Quand devrais-je m'agenouiller et prier la ville, cette grosse B.ite

Qui me N.ique trop vite
Essayant de me faire plier à vivre à NYC

C'est Sodome et Gomorrhe cette folle qui a créé cette M.erde
Mes chemises sont trop justes mes pantalons usés
Je suis coincée à coudre de vieux habits en métaphores nouveau style
Mes chaussures ont des oignons mes semelles trop fines pour marcher

Dieu doit être un gangster !
Mes amours sont réduites à manger du melon assise sur une brique
A siroter de l'eau nuageuse à m'arranger de cette M.erde

Ils disent les occasions terribles,
Musique sans fin, ma carrière est au point mort avant le succès

Je suis ce mac soutenant des poëtruses*
Et toi cet accro du mot cherchant à tirer un coup

Que faire à New York City si ce n'est y être, si ce n'est y vivre
Tu me demandes où est passé l'amour, il est parti quand j'étais petite

NYC te fait tirer sur un flic 41 fois juste pour te venger

Entoure cette date sur ton calendrier
Le 2 mars, marche 2000 fois en vie
Nous nous soulèverons et ferons cette guerre à temps, NYC !!!
* poëtruses dans le sens poetricks=tricks=ruses.
MAIS tricks se rapportent au mot=client dans le jargon de la prostitution.

NYC

Fought obstacles created thru song
Lullaby children running around corn
Without mothers to look over their coming
of age

The silent rage of fathers can be echoed for
days thru the walls of
Sing Sing jail prisons
Unrightful accusations alongside guilty
parishioners

We complain about there being no Kings
around
Immigrants get off the plane and kiss the
ground hearing curse word love poems and
sex proposals
Can I be a millionaire?
The leaves fall off the thorns, the artist start
to draw characters with no tongues/ relaying
false messages of what's your hand doing
crossing "t's" on my face for?

We create sugar artificial drinks to alleviate
the pain
I didn't listen to God when she said "pay
more attention to me"
So my daughters got deaf water in her ear

I salsa, merengue and mambo my summer
daily walks thru the city.
My ears bleed from other people's negativity.

When asked where did the love go, it left
when I was a child.
Playing over crack vials,
jumping rope thru alcoholic glass bottles,
running laps over dead bodies.
My aspirations sway like the tops of trees
hoping one day to break out and climb
higher to achieve

Concrete has become the mask I wear
I'm looking for that special box to lay in
As I beg for a coin or two to buy back my
sanity
Flower petals sit in a glass on top my
creativity

We fast-forward to a page we want to be on
Our books a 1910 Biology
Living in the past,
we assimilate
Kiss ass
Pass tests

All in the name of survival
Living from paycheck to pay check
Is this all that life has for me
Living in New York City

Celebrate Brooklyn they say,
go to Central Park
Get molested and raped
Jogging away your despair
Inhaling pollution and smog everyday

As I'm forced to be one with nature in a box
called park
My instincts leave me in the dark
I paint a picture through $9.50 movies and
stale popcorn
Rats with long tails keep my feet warm

Where I'm gonna go to keep from being torn
apart
People in love argue from the start over what
bills to pay
John White was the one who got the raise
today
When should I get on my knees and pray to

the big city "D" ick
that's "F" ucking me to quick
Trying to get to me to submit to living in
New York City

It's 'Sodom & Gomorrah' that bitty that
created this "s" hit

My shirts too tight my pants too sick
I'm stuck sewing old clothes into
new style metaphors
My shoes have bunions and low
soles to walk on.

God must be a thug!
My loves resorted to eating watermelon on
a brick
Sipping on cloudy water
Putting up with this "s" hit

The opportunities tremendous
Music never ending
My career on standstill within success

I'm that mobster pimping poetricks
You that word addict trying to get a hit

What to do in New York City
just to live just to be in
You ask where did the love go,
it left when I was a child

NYC make you shoot a cop 41
times just/ to retaliate

Mark your calendars remember this date
March you 2 two thousand times alive
We gonna raise up and fight this war on time

New York City!!!

- Kasema Kalifah

RENDEZ-VOUS

Ce que l'oeil a
vu, le coeur ne
l'oublie jamais.

**What the eye has
seen the heart
never forgets.**

-Proverbe-Togo

Rendez-vous Paris

Accorde-moi cette danse et ne dit pas non
« NoN »
Mes mots dansent sur la mélodie de ton
nom « Non »
Même en silence j'ai la mémoire qui tangue
C 'que j'voulais te dire, je l'ai sur l' bout d'
la langue

J'prends mon courage à deux mains, j'me
jette à l'eau
J'ai pas l 'pied marin pour mener les filles
en bateau
Dis-moi...Comment font les hommes pour
vivre sans toi ?
J' ai pas une minute à moi, « pourquoi ? »,
le temps c'est toi !

Un peu comme des jumeaux ton souffle
devient le mien
Ton silence trouve mes mots mon mal «
devient mon bien ! »
J'ai tout mélangé, mais j'n'ai rien perdu,
Dis pas qu'j'me suis trompé, je nous ai «
confondu ! »

Mon coeur s'est arrêté, s'te plaît...rappuie
sur play, referme ma plaie,
tu sais pas qu'tu m'plais ? « tu crois qu'tu
m'connais ?!
Toi et moi, c'est tout et on est au complet...
« Finis ton couplet ! »
Besoin de toi, envie de rien j'te promets
! ! !

Tu m'as rendu « fou »... Accepte mon
rendez-vous
Laisse moi une trace de Lipstick « sur le
cou »
« Tu t'es rendu » fou avec ce Rendezvous

Chut ! J'dirai plus rien puisque tu devines
tout !
(Tais toi !)

J'apprends par coeur chacun des traits qui
te parcourent
Appelle ça comme tu veux, j'crois qu'ça
s'appelle : « L'Amour ? »
Partout autour de moi je retrouve ton
empreinte
Perdu dans un labyrinthe dont je cherche
la feinte.

J'ai l'sens de l'humour au bout du rouleau
Un chagrin d'amour à noyer au bord du
goulot
Le charme est ton arme, j' peux mourir
pour tes lèvres
Pas d'arc-en-ciel sans larmes, tu colories
mes rêves

J't'ai vu à l'oeil nu, et t'ai rêvé dévêtue
J'suis tombé des nues dans un tendre piège
tendu
Touché, par un canon qui m'a mis l' feu ...
« aux poudres »
Mieux, dévalisant le ciel de ses coups
d'foudre

Qu'il serait tendre de t'entendre m'appeler
ton poète,
j' te laisserai descendre sur les maux d'ma
tête
Maîtresse de la beauté tu m'arraches deux
à deux
les perles de mes yeux pour t'en faire un
collier

Tu m'as rendu fou... Accepte mon rendez-
vous
Laisse-moi une trace de Lipstick sur le cou
Tu t'es rendu fou avec ton rendez-vous
Chut ! J'dirai plus rien puisque tu devines
tout

Un ange passe le temps d'avaler un Diab-
olo menthe
T'as l'air de la religieuse qu'on prie de
devenir l' amante
« Les aimants s'attirent, même si c'est bien
au départ
les amants soupirent...et rêvent d'un nouveau départ »

Chaque fois qu'tu pars, y 'a plus nulle part
où aller
J'dépends de tes départs, tu m' laisses un
goût « salé »
Même le jour il fait nuit quand tu n'es pas
là
La terre tourne autour d'elle-même et
n'aime que toi !

Au lieu d'un « bouque »t d' fleurs accepte ce
« bouquet » d'mots
Dont le parfum espère effleurer ta peau,
Je souffle sur le soleil en espérant l'éteindre
M' étends vers ton sommeil « sans jamais
l'atteindre ».

Tu m'as rendu fou... Accepte mon rendez-
vous
Laisse moi une trace de Lipstick sur le cou
Tu t'es rendu fou avec ton rendez-vous
Chut ! J'dirai plus rien puisque tu devines
tout (tais toi)

Rendez-vous Paris

Grant me this dance and don't say "No"
On the melody of your name my words
flow "No"
Even in silence my memory slips
What I wanted to tell you was on the tip of
my lips

I take my courage, join my hands, jump
into water
Hard to lead girls on my boat, I'm no good
sailor
Tell me...how do men manage to live
without you?
Don't have a minute to myself, "Why?"...
'cause time is you!

Seems like twins, your breath becomes
mine
Your silence finds my words, you change
despair into "good times"
I've mixed all up, but didn't lose anything,
Don't say I'm wrong, it's just you and I
confusing.

My heart pushed STOP, come on, hit
PLAY again, heal my pain,
Don't you know I like you? "you think you
know me?"
You and me, that's all, no need of nobody
else..."Finish your verse"
Need you, feel like nothing else, I promise!

Who drives me crazy? "YOU"...accept my
rendez-vous
Leave me a trace of lipstick "sur le cou"*
You turned crazy..."WHO" with this
rendez-vous
Shh! I remain silent since you guess it all,
boo!
Shush! Be quiet!

I learn by heart every smile you leave
Call it whatever but it sounds like "Love?"
Everywhere around me I find your trace
Lost in a maze, all I find out is your face

My sense of humor isn't fun anymore
An unhappy love affair to drown my sorrow in liquor
Charm is your weapon, I could die for you
lips
There's no rainbow without tears, you
color my dreams

Saw you with naked eyes, and dreamed of
you nude
I cannot believe a tender trap is so rude
Got hit by a bomb, you "lit me up"
Better yet, stripped the sky of its thunder-
bolts

How sweet it will be to hear you call me
your poet
I'll let you get down on the ache in my
head
Mistress of beauty, you rip out 2 by 2
The pearls of my eyes make a necklace for
you

Who drives me crazy? "YOU"...accept my
rendez-vous
Leave me a trace of lipstick "sur le cou"
You turned crazy..."WHO" with this
rendezvous
Shh! I remain silent since you guess it all,
boo!

Shush! Be quiet!

I saw an angel while having my Devil
cocktail
You are like the nun we pray to become a
lover, hell (yeah)
"When magnets attract...feels good from
the start
Lovers dream of a new beginnings with a
sigh of the heart"

Each time you leave, there's nowhere else
to go
I depend on your departures, you leave a
"salty" flow
When you aren't there, even daytime feels
blue
The earth revolves around itself, only
loving you!

Instead of a "bunch" of flowers, have this
"bouquet" of words
Whose fragrance would love to brush
against your skin
I blow on the sun, trying to put it out
Stretch into your dream "without reaching it."

* On my neck

- *John Banzaï*

John Banzaï

63

Rendez-vous New-York

Accorde-moi cette danse et ne dit pas non
« Non »
Mes mots dansent sur la mélodie de ton
nom « Non »
Même en silence j'ai la mémoire qui tangue
C'que j'voulais te dire, je l'ai sur l'bout d'
la langue

Sur le fil feel mon fuel funambule ma belle
Si j'te fais mon numéro, c'est pour qu'tu
t'en rappelles
Les cieux se resserrent sérieusement dans
mes yeux
J'me sens l'coeur d'un Icare prêt à défaire
le feu

Le power de ton parfum embaume la pièce
J'sais plus quelle flower est-il quand tu
move tes « yes »
J'deviens long John avec un big 'blème de
drague
Mon tic-tac bug on nage en plein « jet lag »

Hold up ! j'te vole une minute
Pas de panique
Laisse toi détrousser par le gentleman aux
manètes
Vu comme j'flashe faut qu'j'te french kiss
miss
C'est toi la shooting star « qui black-out
ton cosmos »

Tu m'as rendu « fou »
Accepte mon rendez-vous
Laisse-moi une trace de Lipstick « sur le
cou »
Tu t'es rendu « fou »

Avec ton rendez « vous »
Chut
Ecoute j'me tais je sais que tu devines tout
-J'dirai plus rien puisque tu devines tout

Tout me touche, chez toi, jusqu'au bout de
tes doigts
J'n'ai jamais vu des yeux comme ceux-là et
ta bouche « n'en parle pas »
Ça y est j'ai fait mon voeu devant l'défilé
d'étoiles
Te suivre d'assez près pour t'apprendre ma
langue natale

J't'apprendrai « Oh LA LA » tu m'apprends
l'reste « on troque ? »
Tu verras pas b'soin d'fric pour être un
traveler-choc
« Banzaï kick it » Yes I Can !
Pour toi, je ferai de chaque jour de la
semaine un week-end

Read my lips darling when I smile « shin-
ning »
Remember rendez-vous after U à
l'aquaplanning
Pour swimming cool water proof flow
beautiful
Mon Style Vroom dans ta valley drive in
my room

Ma vie un movie en V.O ou l'hiver « se
meurt »
L'été sera Hot fondant comme un Mystère
SISTER
Si j'approche ma bouche c'est pour tête à
tête

Viens j't'emmène au « seventh heaven »
compte jusqu'au « SUNSET »

Tu m'as rendu « fou »
Accepte mon rendez-vous
Laisse-moi une trace de Lipstick « sur le
cou »
Tu t'es rendu « fou »
Avec ton rendez « vous »
Chut
Ecoute j'me tais je sais que tu devines tout
-J'dirai plus rien puisque tu devines tout

« Je dream », do U speak ma langue ?
S'il vous plait lady, do I rewind la bande ?
Est-ce que vous rester fidèle c'est vous
tromper toutes ?
« ce sont ces femmes qui vous consumment
qui sèment le doute ? »

Tes hanches dépassent la marge remplis-
sent mes feuilles blanches
Ce dont j'ai envie : une soif que seule ta
bouche étanche
Tu maîtrises l'arpège jusqu'au bout des
ongles « je joue »
Avec mes sens jongle et mets les sens dessus « dessous »

Souffle lève le vent Love l'over Prose
Parle-moi du silence si ça t'dit quelque
chose
Si j'te retiens c'est juste pour pas que tu
m'oublies
J'te laisse le dernier mot : à Deux commence... « l'infini »

Rendez-vous New-York

Grant me this dance and don't say no-"no"
On the melody of your name my words
flow "no"

Even in silence my memory slips
What I wanted to tell you was on the tip of
my lips

U're my tightrope walker, feel my fuel ma belle
If I give U my number, it's 4 U 2
call my cell
The Skies seriously tighten my eyes
My heart feels like Icarus, ready
to untie fire

The power of your fragrance penetrates
my room
Don't know what flower it is when U move
Ur ...-"yes"
I become long John with a big problem
of chat
My tick-tock crashes, we swim in full "jetlag"

Hold up! I steal a minute from U
Allow U 2 B robbed by the gentleman
in control
See how I flash, I have to French Kiss
U miss
U're the shooting star "that black-out
my cosmos"

Who drives me crazy ? "YOU"...accept my
rendez-vous
Leave me a trace of lipstick "sur le cou"
You turned crazy ... "WHO" with this
rendez-vous
Shh! I remain silent since you guess

it all, boo!
Shush! Be quiet!

All touches me in U, untill Ur fingertips
I've never seen eyes like those and Ur
mouth...- "don't talk about it"
That's it I've made my wish staring at a
parade of stars
2 follow U close enough 2 teach U my
native tongue

I'll teach U: Oh la la, U'll teach me the
rest - "Let's trade"
U see, don't need no money 2 B a
traveler-shock
"Banzaï kick it!" Yes I can!
4 U, I'll make every day a weekend

Read my lips, darling when I smile
– "shining"
Remember Rendez-vous after U at the
Aquaplanning
For swimming pool, waterproof, flow
beautiful
My style hums in Ur valley, drives
in my room

My life a movie in V.O. where winter dies
Summer's gonna B Hot melty like a
sundae sister
If I put my mouth close 2 U, it's 2 B
face 2 face
Come, I bring U 2 "seventh heaven" count
until "sunset"

Who drives me crazy? "YOU"...accept my
rendez-vous
Leave me a trace of lipstick "sur le cou"
You turned crazy ... "WHO" with this
rendez-vous
Shh! I remain silent since you guess it all, boo!
Shush! Be quiet!

I "dream," do U speak my tongue?
Please lady do I rewind the tape?
Being faithful is it cheating on every one
of U?
- "Those are women who consume U who
spread the doubt"

Ur hips enlarge the margin fulfill my
empty pages
What do I need: a thirst that only Ur lips
can appease I know what I want Ur mouth
to become my thirst
U master arpeggio to the tip of Ur nail
With my senses juggle and put it upside–down

Blow, Rise the wind, love the over prose
Tell me about silence if U've heard about it
If I hold U it's 4 U not 2 forget
I leave U the last word: together begins:
"infinity"

- John Banzaï

John Banzaï

If the rhythm of the drum
beat changes, the dance
step must adapt.
-Yoruba proverb

Embrasse moi - Katt II Remix

Quand le rythme du
tambour change, le pas
doit s'adapter.
-Proverbe Yoruba

PROSE ELECTRIQUE PART 2

Qu'est-ce qu'aimer sinon reconnaître en l'autre
la part de son être qui le tire de l'ombre,
qui le tire au dessus de lui-même et le sauve de
la médiocrité.

**What is it to love, if not the recognition
that part of one's being rises above himself,
takes him out of the shadows and saves him
from mediocrity.**

-Henry James

On dit qu'il y a dans l'alphabet
tous les parfums et toutes
les saveurs, tous les bruits et
toutes les formes, toutes les
matières et toutes les couleurs.

They say that the alphabet
contains every perfume, every
flavor, every sound, every
material and every color.

-SD

PROSE ÉlEctriquE – Part 2

Rêve d'une autre Rive

L'encre en mouillage capturait ses voy-
ages...
Son plus grand admirateur la projetait
agrandie, et répétait ses flashes comme un
bègue intimidé par ses propres songes. Je
...revois...
L'insaisissable cambrioleuse sans effrac-
tion, derrière la vitrine d'une bijouterie :
D' émeraude...elle aime rôder
Diamant...on se dit amants
Saphir... s'affirmer...
Accompagner ta solitude accepter de tout
perdre, tout de suite...
Franchir le pont où les ombres se tra-
versent...Traverser les ombres où les ponts
se franchissent
Elle lit derrière mon épaule la vie devant
nous
Reflet incertain ...mon miroir a perdu son
teint , j' peux plus scruter les traits d' mon

visage immobile comme un cadran solaire,
si t'es l'heure qui m' tourne autour...
tu m'épuises in-fa-ti-ga-ble-ment –teuse
! ! !
Dépêche-toi d' me comprendre avant qu' le
halo qui nous éclaire ne fige mon expression en grimace. C'qui nous unit c'est ce
sol... entraînant le cortège de nos pensées
contradictoires...

Tu flottes « Je flotte »...l'onde s'est noyée
dans son élément , tu t'es perdue dans ma
rétine,
mon ombre aveugle se repose au cré-
puscule où d'irréconciliables nombres se
frôlent, frileux couples infidèles , mon
loyal adversaire mesure la promenade aux
enjambées qui s'articulent.

Le sommeil me réclame, pour alimenter
ses rêves
et la réalité se démultiplie alors

sous l'ombrelle où on brûle paranoïaque
l'immortelle suicidaire
Moi et ma sombre ombre...Elle et son lit
vide

Ton absence m'éclaire, j'ai saisi ,j' te sais
irréelle, mais j'ai rompu avec...ma lucidité,
celle même qui t'a fait fuir en te rappelant
qu'une femme au foyer brûle à petit feu...

J'me répète son passage X fois...et mon
ombre fétiche reste : Zéro, en ce qu'elle ne
fut jamais mienne.

J'ai volé l'ombre d'une passante, (la tienne
dormait dessous)
pour dérober un peu d'amour
à la vitesse de la lumière
à la lueur d'un réverbère
branché sur ma prose électrique.

John Banzaï

ElEctric ProsE – Part 2

Dream of another shore

Watered-down ink captured her journeys...
Her biggest admirer projected her even
bigger, and repeated the flashes of light
like a stammer intimidated by his own
thoughts. My mind goes back... The elusive
no-break-in-lady-burglar behind the
window of a jewelry store:
Emerald... Come, hold
Diamond... Won't die
Sapphire... Self fire
Following her loneliness agreeing to lose
everything, right away...
Cross the bridge where the shadows go
through
"Go through the shadows where the bridges
cross"
She reads over my shoulder the life ahead
of us
"Unsure reflection"...my mirror changed
complexion, I can't scan anymore the

features on my face static as a sundial, if
you are time ticking around me...
You wear me out « un »-Tir-« ring »-Lea-
ve-me!!!
Hurry up and understand me before the
halo illuminating us freezes my expressions into a frown. What unites us is this
ground...dragging the cortege of our fight-
ing thoughts...

You float..."I float"...The wave is drowned
in its own element, you got lost in my
retina, my blind shadow rests at twilight,
where irreconcilible numbers brush
against each other, overcautious unfaithful
couples, my loyal opponent measures the
walk with strides of my talk.

Sleep asks for me, to feed its dream
And reality then drops
Under the parasol where we burn paranoid
immortal suicide...

Me and my dark shadow... Her and her
empty bed...

Your absence enlightens me, I feel... you're
unreal... but I broke up with... my lucidity,
the same one that drove you away, reminding you that a woman at home simmers.

I repeat her come-and-go X times... and
my favorite number is still: nil, coz' she
was never mine!

I stole the shadow of a passerby, "yours
were sleeping under her"
To snatch a little love
At the speed of light
By the glow of a city lamp
Hooked up to my « prose électrique ».

- John Banzaï

Lovestories

Des hommes et des femmes ...

Just give the time to discover you
To taste every inch of your skin
To engrave my smile onto the ebony
depths of your pupils
To fill your heart and body with the
most unforgettable essences
Let me penetrate your soul
Timeless moments
Wherein lie the mysteries of love.

Laisse-moi seulement le temps
de te découvrir
De goûter chaque inch de ta peau
De graver mon sourire dans l'èbène
de tes pupilles
D'impregner ton coeur et ton corps de
la plus inoubliable des essences
Laisse-moi pénétrer ton âme.
Moments intemporels
Là où résident les mystères
de l'amour.

Helene - In love.

They say that butterflies are flowers, which
learned to fly by flapping their petals.
+ + × × + + × × × + × + × + × + + × × + + × × × × + × + × +
On dit que les papillons sont des fleurs qui
ont appris à voler en battant des pétales.

-Helene Faussart

To The Queen

Les contes de fées se renouvellent toujours
sans que toujours pourtant nos cœurs
soient assez simples et assez purs pour
les accepter.

-Henry James

Pour La Reine

Tu me rappelles ces Reines dont je suis
tombé amoureux
Lorsque d'un oeil culturel je vis les fidèles
peintures des héroïnes de mon histoire
J'aurais aimé pouvoir bâtir des monuments
pour toi
Et pénétrer dans les cités par les arches de
tes jambes hautes de 30 pieds
J'aurais ciselé ton visage à l'intérieur de
mon temple
Et honoré l'autel de ta lèvre inférieure
J'aurais laissé des offrandes sur le bout de
ta langue
Et incliné ma tête en prière avant que tu me...
Excuse-moi.......J'ai dit ça ?
Ou est-ce tout ce que j'ai dit ?
Je voulais dire
Que j'aurais tagué ton nom dans le ciel
Sur cette voie lactée comme un dieu b-boy
amoureux
Mais c'est pas vraiment mon style
Et flatter tes yeux ou ton sourire
Semble si insignifiant
Tant ta splendeur est magique
Et mérite tellement mieux que moi
Moi qui ne peux faire qu'essayer

De rassembler mon courage pour
t'approcher
Comme un ado sur le point de demander
l'autographe
De sa star de ciné préférée
Tu me rappelles l'apparition de cette étoile
que l'on pourrait presque toucher
Et qui s'enfuit l'instant d'après plus loin
sans doute que j'imagine
Mais dont la lueur scintille assez encore
pour éclairer la pièce
Une étoile que seuls les sages suivraient
Et comme une étoile je sens ma destinée
quelque part plongée dans la tienne
Mais je ne peux le prouver

Ma Reine je brûle de ce désir
Pourquoi ne pas plonger ces doigts dans ta
matière
Et n'en rafraîchir que ma langue
Et mettre au monde mes petits
Et écouter les chants que j'aurais bien
laissé chanter au céleste gardien
Puisque tu es la plus belle créature qu'il
m'ait été donné de voir
Et de ne pas avoir

Ma Reine, puis-je troubler une parcelle de
ton temps
Lequel est si précieux qu'il élude le temps
et n'en prend aucun dans mon espace
Car ta place sera celle que tu souhaites
Et mon seul espoir est que tu m'en gardes
une
Que tu te souviennes
Comme je ne peux oublier ces temps où on
s'est rencontré
Parce que c'était plus d'une fois
Et une fois pour toutes devint il était une
fois
Quand mon imaginaire se glissa dans ma
réalité
Et le fit si innocemment
Ma Reine
Arrivé là, « je t'aime » ressemble à un
balbutiement d'idiot
Mais l'élan lui ne bégaie pas
Le coeur palpite comme les papillons se
posent sur des fleurs belles comme toi
Juste pour en recueillir le sucre .

Jamarhl Crawford

To The Queen

You remind me of the Queens I fell in
Love with
When I first saw culturally accurate depic-
tions of my historical she-roes
I wish I could build monuments to you
And enter cities through the arches of
your 30-foot legs
I would chisel your face on the inside of
my temple
And worship at the altar of your bottom lip
I would leave offerings on the tip of your
tongue
And bow my head in prayer before you...
Excuse me... did I say that?
Or is that all I said
I meant to say
That I would skywrite your name in graffiti
Across the milky way like a b-boy god in
love
But that's really not my style
And complimenting your eyes or your
smile
Seems so insignificant
When you are so magically magnificent
And deserve so much more than I

When all I can do is try
To muster up the audacity to approach you
Like a schoolboy fan about to solicit an
autograph
From his favorite female movie star
You remind me of a star appearing close
enough to touch
And still shining bright enough to light a
room
A star that wise men would follow
And like a star I feel that my destiny is
somehow wrapped in you
But I can't prove it

My Queen, I am burning with desire
Would you not dip yourself of yourself
And cool but my tongue
And bear my young
And listen to songs that i would much
rather have sung by the heavenly host
Because you are the most beautiful crea-
ture I have ever beheld
And never held
My Queen, could I trouble you for a
moment of your time

Which is so valuable it eludes time and
takes up no time in my space
Because your place is wherever you wish
it to be
And my only hope is that you somehow
include me
Remember me
I cannot forget the times we met
Because it was more than once
And all at once became once upon a time
When my fantasy stepped into my reality
And did so innocently
My Queen at this point "I Love You" seems
like the simple utterings of an idiot
But my feelings don't stutter
Heart flutters like butterflies who land on
beautiful flowers like you
Only to partake of sweet nectars.

- Jamarhl Crawford

Untitled Rhapsody

✗✗+✗✗✗+ +✗✗+✗✗✗✗+✗+✗✗+✗✗ ✗ +✗✗✗+✗✗+✗✗✗✗✗+✗✗
+✗✗✗+✗✗✗✗✗+✗✗

Rhapsodie Sans Nom

mon amant me couvrira de musique
ses mots, notes tombant doucement autour
de nous
comme des rafales de neige scintillante
par un jour d'hiver ensoleillé
du bout des doigts il tapote des sections
rythmiques
sur mon dos, expirations mélodiques
contre mon oreille, en cadence
tel le métronome que nos pas créent
alors que nous faisons la traversée mains
jointes
pour unir plusieurs tribus africaines
et quelques contrées européennes
en une parfaite composition harmonique

j'ai des visions d'amour grandioses
des symphonies jouées par de grands
orchestres
au sommet des montagnes pendant qu'une
diva gueule du gospel
et que le choeur du tabernacle
proclame notre amour à la Terre
comme au Ciel et même ceux pourvus de
sourdes oreilles

peuvent le goûter dans l'air
après l'amour, même ceux qui ne nous con-
naissent pas se sentent
étrangement et soudainement
comme s'ils venaient de finir un bon repas
ou d'avoir une conversation excitante sur
l'existence

peut être que je vise trop haut
mais j'aspire à un amour digne d'une
superbe soirée
un amour plein d'âme et 'groovy', de celui
qui donne envie
aux gens de s'y rassembler
et de danser
un amour si passionné que
des petits villages
se blotissent autour de nous pour
s'imprégner de notre chaleur
entraînés dans une fête incontrôlable
de nous, célébration

je voudrais être aimée
avec une telle puissance que je sois repous-
sée

par le toucher de n'importe lequel et par
celui de tous les autres hommes
un amour qui magnifie si intensément mes
sens
que je puisse encore sentir son aura
des heures après qu'il ait quitté ma
chambre
musc égyptien et sueur profondément
imprégnés
sur ma taie d'oreiller

mon amant m'enveloppera
d'un arc-en-ciel de rimes pendant que les
mouettes chanteront en arrière-plan
et que les phoques joueront des solos sexy
de saxophone
sur des plages de sable noir
notre remix d'un air ancien et éternel
tellement funky que
Dieu elle-même
S'arrêtera dans son oeuvre pour écouter le
groove
Et dire : « Hé mais... c'est ma chanson ! »

Nazelah Jamison

Untitled Rhapsody

my lover will cloak me in music,
his words, notes falling softly around us
like snow flurries, bright
on a sunny winter day
fingertips tapping rhythm section
on my back, melodic exhalations
against my ear, kept in time to
the metronome our footsteps create
as we walk across, hands clasped to
unite several african tribes
and a few european countries
in perfect harmonic composition

i have colossal visions of love
symphonies played by large orchestras
on mountain tops, while diva belts gospel
tunes and the tabernacle choir
proclaims our love to the heavens
and the earth, and even those who own
deaf ears
can taste it in the air
after our lovemaking people who
don't even know us will oddly and
suddenly feel

as if they've just finished a good meal
or a stimulating conversation about
existence

perhaps my sights are lofty
but i yearn for a love like 'the supper club'
a love so soulful and groovy as to cause
many groups of people to want to gather
and dance to it
so passionate as to attract
small villages
huddled around us for warmth
caught up in the uncontrollable gala
celebration of us

i want to be loved with a force
so powerful that i am repulsed
by any and every other man's touch
that so intensively magnifies my senses
that i still smell his aura
hours after he's left my room
egyptian musk oil and sweat soaking deep
into my pillowcase

my lover will wrap me up
in rhyme rainbows while seagulls sing
background
and seals play sexy saxophone solos
on black sand beaches
our new mix of an ancient and timeless
tune
so funky as to cause
god herself
to look up from what she's doing to catch
the groove
and say, "Hey...that's my song!"

- Nazelah Jamison

Je Te Souhaite Une Blanche Nuit

Ecoute je t'aime
Listen I love you
Comme on meurt
the way we die
Innocemment, totalement
Innocently, totally
et je t'attendrai comme le bonheur
And I'll wait for you like happiness
tous les jours.
Every day

Patrice Kayo

Je Te Souhaite Une Blanche Nuit

Approche et montre moi ta peau, mets ta plus belle tenue d'Eve

En attendant que le jour se lève nous allons faire le même rêve

J'aimerais te voir t'offrir, seulement vêtue d'un sourire

J'aimerais t'entendre chanter la mélodie de tes plus beaux soupirs

Partons pour ce voyage très long

Et je ferais l'effort pour que tu t'en souviennes comme de ton prénom

Je suis venu boire à l'eau de ton puits

Je suis venu pour te voir suer comme tombe la pluie

J'ai collé ta photo derrière mes paupières et c'est merveilleux

Je peux te voir même quand je ferme les yeux

J'irais chercher tes plaisirs et demain il t'en restera encore

Je te trouve belle comme un astre en or

Approche et montre moi ton autre toi

Cette nuit il va y avoir un tremblement de terre juste sous notre toit

Souleymane Diamanka

I Wish You A Sleepless Night

Come closer and show me your skin, put on your finest
Eve's dress

While we wait for daybreak we'll dream the same dream

I'd like you to give yourself to me wearing nothing but a smile

I'd like to hear you sing the melody of your finest sighs

Let's take this very long journey

And I'll make an effort, for you to remember just like
your name

I came to drink water from your well

I stuck your picture behind my eyelids and it's wonderful

I can see you even when my eyes are closed

I'll go look for your pleasures and tomorrow there'll be some
left for you still

I think you're as beautiful as a golden star

Come closer and show me your other self

Tonight there's gonna be an earthquake right under our roof.

- Souleymane Diamanda

Art is a celebration of life even when life extends to death.

-Ralph Ellison

The Death and the Living

La Mort et le Vivant

Elle a vécu deux ans à l'orée d'elle-même
Hébétée et perdue
Il fallut deux mouchoirs pour sécher ses
pleurs
Deux bières ont noyé ses craintes
En fait elle les déguisait
Ce qui était plutôt mieux
Car si elle se regardait dans les yeux
Voyant son propre reflet
C'est un peu d'elle-même qui mourrait

Elle repète « ça va », mais nous savons tous
que c'est un mensonge
Au fond d'elle même le spleen la ronge
Se rappelant le passé à chaque fois qu'elle
se déshabille
Elle se souvient des longues nuits la tête
sur sa poitrine
Pendant qu'il murmurait passionnément
« Bébé tu es unique, je veux que jamais on
n'se sépare »

Ils vivaient à Brownsville depuis le départ
Fréquentèrent les mêmes écoles, elle lui
offrit son coeur, il en fit de même
Il lui apprit les maths et de son nom,
étudia l'origine même

Qu'est-ce qu'un Dieu peut faire pour
changer

Une Reine en demande spirituelle
Affirmer que le divin est présent à chaque
instant

Ils étaient comme deux flammes unis en
un cierge éblouissant aveu
Brûlant intensément en un combat sacré
Pour que les Dieux les détruisent
Et que les démons les haïssent
C'est drôle, mais elle sait que tu es proche
Quand le coeur saute dans sa coquille
jusqu'au matin suivant
Quand le Soleil endort la Terre dans une
tempête universelle
Elle réalise que la norme n'est plus la
même qu'avant

Elle entend tes pas sur le parquet
Et peut sentir ton énergie enveloppant ses
épaules
Avec la chaleur de trois millions de soldats
Sur le sentier de la guerre en route pour
la paix

Tu la fais pleurer
Quand elle réalise que c'est toi qui écrit ce
poème
Et rien ni personne ne pourra empêcher
Nos transmissions de pensée que seul
l'esprit connaît

Et elle se demande pourquoi il fallut la
mort pour que les unions du premier
regard se rejoignent

Tu vois comme disait mon frère
Alpha et Oméga pratiquent le Yin et le
Yang
Conscience spirituelle
Elle écrit maintenant sans réfléchir
et sa main touche son visage avec majesté
mais rien n'a changé
Elle lévite sans quitter son corps
Elle peut sentir ses lèvres au bas de sa
nuque
Comme les rayons du soleil

Les soupirs maintenant ne viennent plus
des poumons
Mais de son âme

Ça c'est l'amour

Qui a dit que deux être ne pouvaient
s'aimer en étant séparés

La Mort et le Vivant

Kasema Kalifah

The Death And The Living

She's been living on the outskirts of
herself for 2 years
Dazed and confused
It took 2 tissues to dry her tears
2 beers concealed her fears
actually gave her a disguise
which was kind of cool cus
every time she looked in her eyes
able to see herself
clearly a part of her would die

Saying to herself it's cool but we all know
it's a lie
Deep down inside she's depressed
Constantly reminded of her past every
time she gets undressed

She remembers the long nights she would
hold his head upon her chest
While he whispered passionately
*"baby you're the best, and I
don't ever want us to be apart"*

They lived in Brownsville from the start
Went to the same schools and she gave him
her heart and shortly after he did the same
Taught her the mathematics and the
breakdown of her righteous name

What a God can do to change
A Queen with the spiritual claims
that the divine exists in out first-eye
windowpanes

Were like two flames inside one white
candle glare
burning vibrantly in a spiritual warfare
For Gods to destroy
and Demons to hate
Funny but she knows you're near
when the heart of her shell jumps at the
a.m. of the next day
When the Sun sleeps the Earth into a
universal storm
She realizes the norm ain't what it used
to be.

She hears your footprints on the wooden
floor
And can feel your energy surrounding her
shoulders
With the heat of 3 billion soldiers
on a warpath for peace

See you bring her to tears
when she realizes you're the one writing
this piece
And nothing anyone could do would

separate
our mental speaks in tongues only the
spiritual can eat
And she wonders why it took death to join
first-eye unions

You see like my brother said
Alpha and Omega be operating yin & yang
Spiritual consciousness
She writes now without thought
and her hand touches her face in similar
King ways
but nothing's changed
She levitates without leaving the body
and can feel his lips on the back of her
neck
Like sun Rays

Exhales now come from the soul
Instead of the lungs

This is love

Who said love can't exist on two planes

The Death & the Living.

- Kasema Kalifah

Human Spiritual
Nature

Les éléments

Ecoute plus souvent
Les choses que les êtres
La voix du feu s'entend
Entends la voix de l'eau
Ecoute dans le vent
Le buisson en sanglot
C'est le souffle des ancêtres.

Listen more
To things than to words that are said
The water's voice sings
and the flame cries
and the wind that brings the
wood sighs
It's the breathing of the ancestors

-Birago Diop

Nous ressusciterons nos morts !
Et qu'ils soient célébrés aux quatre rives de notre diaspora !
Porte au loin ma chanson
Dowore
Fructifie ma querelle
Longue encore est la nuit que nous veillons
Longue et longue
Et je ne dois pas me tromper.

WHEN THE SKY BURST INTO TEARS

We shall revive our dead! Let them be known on
the four banks of the Diaspora!
Carry my song far away
Dowore
Let my quarrel bear fruit
Long is the night we keep watch
So, so long
And I must not be wrong

Bernard Zadi Zaourou

Quand Le Ciel Eclate En Sanglots (Orage, eau des espoirs)

Écoute comme le vent a la voix grave quand il chante l'orage
Bientôt les larmes du ciel vont pleuvoir sur nos visages, la nuit va être sauvage
Tous aux abris ma soeur, préviens nos vieillards et nos ados
Le tonnerre va se mettre dans une colère noire
Et gronder l'homme comme s'il s'était mis les éléments de la nature à dos
Écoute la foudre, écoute ce bruit vivant qui éclaire les nuits les plus sombres
Et vois comme sa lumière étrangle le silence et déchire les ombres
Écoute ces nuages à la peau grise qui bombent le torse, qui crient et qui crachent du feu de toutes
leurs forces
Leur souffle épineux pique les arbres et leur écorche l'écorce
C'est le ciel qui éclate en sanglots
Et c'est tellement violent qu'on dirait qu'il coule du sang de l'eau
A croire que cette méchante pluie c'est un chagrin qui descend de là-haut
J'ai mesuré l'ampleur des dégâts ma soeur, c'est une catastrophe
Et c'est peut-être pour ça que je reprends mon souffle à peu près toutes les quatre strophes
C'est le ciel qui éclate en sanglots
Et c'est tellement violent qu'on dirait qu'il coule du sang de l'eau
Le vent s'est levé pour que la tempête le voie debout
Et du bout des lèvres il fredonne l'air des charmeurs de torrents de boue
Qui mettent les chambres du progrès en désordre
A croire que c'est la nature qui rappelle à l'homme que c'est elle qui donne les ordres
Parfois je me demande pourquoi il fait si froid dans le coeur des gens
c'est peut-être que quand ils regardent leur âge ils se disent « déjà ? »
Ou peut-être qu'être heureux dans cette société c'est d'être amoureux d'une fille de joie
Quand le vent s'engouffre dans les failles du silence ça ressemble A des hurlements de loup
Et il pleut comme si l'océan s'était assis au-dessus de nous
C'est le ciel qui éclate en sanglots
Et c'est tellement violent qu'on dirait qu'il coule du sang de l'eau.

Souleymane Diamanka

When The Sky Burst Into Tears (Storm, water of hopes)

Listen how the wind's voice is deep when it sings of storms
Soon the heaven's tears will rain on our faces, the night will
Be wild
Head for shelter, everyone, warn the old people and the teens
The thunder will fly into a rage
And scold humankind as if they had turned the nature's elements
against them
Listen to the lightning, this lively sound that brightens the
darkest nights
See how the light strangles silence and tears shadows
Listen to these grey-skinned clouds puffing out their chests,
they shout and spit fire with all their power
Their thorny breaths prick the trees and bark their bark
'cause the sky bursts into tears
It's so violent you'd think blood's running from the water
You'd think this nasty rain was sorrow descending from above
I weighed the extent of the damage, sister it's a catastrophe
And maybe that's why I catch my breath every four verses
'cause the sky bursts into tears
It's so violent you'd think blood's running from the water
The wind rose up so the storm could see it standing
And it half-heartedly hums the tune of mud charmers
That turns chambers of progress upside down
You'd think that Mother Nature's reminding humankind that she
gives the orders
Sometimes I wonder why it's so cold inside people's hearts
Maybe because when they look at their age they say "already?"
Or maybe being happy in this society is like being in love with a woman of easy virtue
When the wind rushes into the rifts of silence it sounds like
wolf howlings
And it rains as if the ocean was sitting on top of us
'cause the sky bursts into tears
It's so violent you'd think blood's running from the water.

- Souleymane Diamanka

The mixture of the marvelous and the terrible is the basic condition of human life and the persistence of human ideals represents the marvelous pulling itself up out of the chaos of the universe. In the fairy tale, beauty must awakened by the beast, the beasty man can only regain his humanity through love....

-Ralph Ellison

FIRE

One piece of green
wood is enough to
stop the other
burning.

Un seul morceau de
bois vert suffit à
empêcher les autres
de brûler.

-Proverbe-Brésil

Le Feu

Y'a l'feu dans mes yeux
Et je n'peux pas pleurer
Mes larmes sont taries
Je me demande pourquoi je vis

Douleur et tristesse brûlent dessous ma chair
Pitié, délivrez ma peau de sa violence
incendiaire
N'avoir jamais été soldat du feu est mon seul
pêché
Alors qu'mon âme se consume comme un
briquet
Et j'crache de l'essence
Je saigne du kérosène
La vaseline même ne saurait soulager mes
plaies
L'âme meurtrie
L'esprit anéanti
Le corps se fait las et usé
Reflet méprisé
Mais tu sais fils, même la mort un jour est
née
Et j'suis en feu !

Ils disent "houla menteuse, elle est amou-
reuse!"

Elle est si chaude que même son futal flambe.
Mais le monde semble avoir oublier
Que quand j'l'ai eu il était déjà bien cramé
Que quand j'l'ai mis il sentait déjà la fumée
Et même maintenant j'peux pas empêcher
Qu'il grésille
Il n'y a même pas de bruine
Quand ton âme se consume
Ma bouche si sèche qu'elle en écume
Même mes paroles se dissipent en brume
Parfois j'aimerais être un garçon pour pou-
voir mouiller mes
Rêves
Mais j'pense pas qu'tu comprennes
J'pense pas qu'tu comprennes c'que j'dis
Quand j'dis qu'il faut
Du liquide à mes pensées pour lubrifier mon
existence
Même mise à sec, d'la résistance
Pour refroidir la persistance
D'une âme calcinée
Et d'un esprit qui brûle
D'éviter la déshydratation
J'en ai marre de cette foutue attente
Alors que les fluides on les balance
Aux égouts de ceux qui n'peuvent même pas

Mesurer les pluies salvatrices
C'est pourquoi,
Je dois attendre en vain...
Et pendant tout ce temps,
Je veux juste « chanter sous la pluie ! »
Pendant que Mère Nature
Soulage les meurtrissures
De mon cerveau et de mon dos
Pendant que de prétendus démons craquent
l'allumette
Qui cramera mon esprit
Arrachent le flow de mes mots
Brûlent une croix qu'il me faut porter
Me font hurler si fort qu'ils m'entendent
S'assurent que je suis réveillée
Juste pour que j'le sente
Et j'suis en feu !
Au feu ! au feu ! au feu !

Mais nous n'avons pas besoin d'eau
Laisse brûler ! laisse brûler ! bébé
« nous n'avons pas besoin d'eau »
Devient l'hymne national de toutes mes filles
et fils
Ca n'y fera rien mais transmettra ces brûlures
à chacun

Nubian Voyager

Queen GodIS

Comme j'les ai accouchés en propageant mes
flammes en un
Feu furieux
Et c'est encore moi qu'ils admirent
Et pendant c'temps, je prie le réservoir des
dieux de venir me
Sauver
Car je n'veux pas haïr toujours cette âme que
Dieu m'a donné
Alors je vous supplie de me baigner dans les
eaux de la Terre
Car je brûle de l'intérieur depuis que je donne
la vie
Bénédiction ou foutue malédiction ?
On m'avait dit que tout était ordre divin
depuis le jour de ma
Conception
Ou devrais-je surgir de ce feu, renaissant tel
le Phoenix ?
La bénédiction
La leçon
Et tout c'que j'peux faire c'est disparaître
Réaliser que j'suis si sacrément mortelle
Que j'peux botter le cul du diable !
Parce que j'suis en feu !
Au feu ! au feu ! au feu !

Et j'me déchaîne comme un brasier
J'suis en feu et j'pourrais bien vous brûler
J'vous l'ai dit déjà
J'peux plus supporter ça
Et j'pourrais vous raser comme le tapis des
forêts
Le serait par un feu de brousse
Le genre qui t'fait passer l'envie du feu
Qui t'fait hurler qu't'en a assez du feu
Tellement je suis le feu
Et j'm'arrête
Pendant qu'tu roules et qu'tu décroches
Et j'm'en grille encore
Comme j'l'ai déjà dit alors
La flamme dans ma tête brûle un feu qui
s'étend
Telle une torche je vous éclaire
Et vous donne de quoi vous nourrir
Contrairement aux morts-vivants
J'continue à vous faire parler
Crachant des flows si brûlants
Que ma salive doit roussir
Mais quand mon âme s'embrase
Y en a qui voudraient m'entraîner là dedans
Vous voudriez essayer de solder mon soleil
Pour en tirer quelques rayons
Pour de l'argent

N'importe quand
Vous voudriez essayer et vendre mon âme
Comme si le feu de mon esprit pouvait
s'échanger pour de
L'or
J'le crois pas trop
Pas pour de l'H2o
Ni pour la moindre trace de froid
Car si vous essayer d'sortir mon feu
Ou de faire pâlir mon éclat
Mon esprit crachera un flow si chaud
Qu'il viendra brûler vos cerveaux comme du
charbon
car mes paroles sont étincelles
Je brille même à travers la nuit
Pour moi s'élever c'est incendier
Ou consumer
Puisque bébé
Mes tâches de sueurs laissent des cendres
Et mes larmes s'écoulent en poussière
Parce que j'suis en feu !
Au feu ! au feu ! au feu !

- Queen GodIs

Fire

Fire in my eyes
And I can't cry
My tears are dry
I wonder why I'm living

Pain and sadness burn beneath my flesh
Please undress my skin from this arsonist
within
My only sin is that I was never ever
a firefighter
Instead my soul burns on like a lighter,
And I bleed kerosene
I spit up gasoline
Not even vaseline can soothe these wounds
Spirit bruised
Mind confused
Body been used and worn
Image so damn scorned
Even death is born, son
And I'm on Fire!

They call me "Liar, Liar pants on Fire"
But this world has seemed to have forgotten
These pants were already burnt when I got
them
Smelled like smoke when I rocked them

And even still I can not stop them –
From sizzling
There ain't even no drizzling
When your soul's burnt out
Mouth so dry you be spitting up drought
And even my flows evaporate into steam
Sometimes I wish I was a boy just so I could
have a wet dream...
But I don't think you understand what I
mean
I don't think you understand what I mean
When I say that I need
Liquid thoughts to lubricate my existence
Even watered down resistance
To extinguish the persistance
Of a soul that burns
And a mind that yearns
To escape dehydration

I am tired of all this damn waiting
While fluids just be wasting
Down the drains of those who ain't
even appreciating
The rains of salvation
And so,
I must be waiting in vain...

And all the while,
I just want to be "singing in the rain!"
While mother nature's blessing
Relieves the stress
From in my brain and in my back
While those who pretend to be devils
strike the match
To cremate my spirit
Take the flow out of my lyrics
Burn a cross so I can wear it
Make me SCREAM so they could hear it
And then they try and make sure I'm awake
Just so I can feel it
And I'm on Fire!
Fire! Fire! Fire!

But we don't need no water
Let it burn! Let it burn, baby!
"We don't need no water"...
Becomes the national anthem for all my
daughters – and my sons
Could not help but pass on these burns to
each one
As I birthed them by spreading my flames
like wildfire
And still it's me that they admire

Nubian Voyager

Queen GodIS

And all the while, I'm praying to the reservoir gods to come and save me
'Cause I don't always want to hate this soul that God gave me
So please bathe me in the waters of the earth
I have been burning at the core since I've been given birth
Is this a blessing or a damn curse?
'Cause I was told that this was all supposed to be in divine order since the first day… of my conception
Or should I be rising through this fire like the phoenix resurrection?
The blessing
The lesson
And all I can do is pass
Realize that I'm so damn hot
That I can kick the devil's ass!
'Cause I'm on Fire!
Fire! Fire! Fire!

And I'm raging just like an inferno
I'm on fire and I might just burn you
I done told you before

Can't take this no more
And I'ma take you out like the whole forest floor
Just like brush-Fire
The type that makes you hush-Fire
Make you scream you had enough!-Fire
And so I stop
While you roll and drop
And then I burn some more
Like I said before
The flame that's in my head burns like how a fire spreads
Like a torch, I give you light
or some food to keep you fed
Unlike the dead-men walking
Instead I keep you talking
I be spitting flows so hot
My saliva must be scorching
But when my soul's ablaze
Some of y'all try to take me through this phase
You try and sell my sunlight
Just so you could get a "rays"
Just for pay
Any day
You try and sell my soul
As if the Fire in my spirit can be traded in for gold

Not for H_2O
Or even a little trace of cold
If you try and put out my Fire
If you try and faint my glow
My mind will spit a flow so hot
It will burn your mentals
Like charcoal in a dark hole
I spark flows
I even shine through at night - "bling bling"
For me to wake up is to ignite
or Combust
'Cause baby,
My sweat stains leave ashes
And my teardrops leave dust
Because I am on FIRE!
FIRE! FIRE! FIRE!

- Queen GodIs

Take the five notes simple and sincere that once Edimo
    Stole from Ngosso; Do not sing the stranger's hope
Sing your own despair
        On the notes of hopes
Covered with sighs and tears

    Sing in the evening of the dance
            And like the dew
On the fresh grass

    On the morning of the feast
        Dance barefooted
on the dead grass of the West

Trample underfoot the carpet scorched
by the still-oppressive sun

    Of an age outworn.

Prends cinq notes
   Sincères et sans fard
qu'autrefois Edimo
   arracha à Nguesso ;
Ne chante pas l'espoir de l'étranger
   Chante ton désespoir
   Sur des mots d'espérance
Couverts de pleurs et de soupirs ;
   Chante au soir de la danse,
Et comme la rosée
   sur l'herbe fraîche
du matin de la fête,
   Danse pieds nus
sur l'herbe morte du couchant,
   Et foule aux pieds
Le tapis brûlé par le soleil encore accablant
   D'une époque fatiguée.

-Francis Bebey

Celia – Les Nubians

Helene – Les Nubians

1 Disagree

Have you ever imagined
Your life going on this way
You run and run
Stressed and worried every day
Babylon tries to drive you crazy
Do you agree with this?

I don't
Coz' no one and nothing can bind my mind
Spirit is worth more than material
That's why I'm free
And I disagree

Evil inspires human spirit
To do his deadly work
You cry and cry
See them selling crack to your black brothers
Babylon tries to kill your blood
Do you agree with this?

I don't
Coz' this is an extermination plan

But black people is protected by Jah
I'm proud and strong
And I disagree

Every day people die
Killed for the pride of Babylon system
Money tries to rule the world
And everything that lives within
Can't you see that things must change
Things must change
THE CHANGE.

You're not the weak one
You are powerful
So don't stay blind
Take a step on the way of consciousness
You must be proud and free
And disagree
You'd better disagree
Just disagree.

- Les Nubians

LA PROSE DES VENTS

On dit que les anges chantent
à l'oreille du poète. SD

**They say that the angels sing
in the poet's ears.**

La Prose Des Vents

C'était une nuit de pleine dune sur les terres arides du Sahel
Le désert était très agité et le paysage indécis
D'immenses statues de sable chevauchaient des brises nerveuses
Et ensemble elles se jetaient sur moi quand je les regardais dans les yeux
C'était une nuit de pleine dune sur les terres arides du Sahel
Mon stylo avait mauvaise mine et la soif me déchirait les lèvres
J'errais comme un damné pourtant je n'étais pas perdu
J'errais comme un damné et je cherchais la prose des vents
C'était une nuit de pleine dune sur les terres arides du Sahel
J'étais debout sur les vagues d'un Sahara en pleine tempête
Et je cherchais ce poème écrit de la main de Dieu.

Souleymane Diamanka

Wind Prose

It was a full dune night on the arid land of Sahel
The desert so agitated and the landscape was uncertain
Huge statues of sand straddled nervous breezes
And together they threw themselves on me when I looked them in the eye
It was a full dune night on the arid land of Sahel
My pen had no well and thirst tore at my lips
I wandered like a damned person although I wasn't lost
It was a full dune night on the arid land of Sahel
I was standing on the waves of the Sahara in full storm
And I was looking for this poem written by the hand of God.

- Souleymane Diamanka

OUTRO:

A book is like a garden in the pocket. Truthland

Un livre est comme un jardin au fond d'une poche.

Book. Read
Feed me
With words
Sentences
Ideas
Experiences
Discoveries
With these strange
Unknown
Pages
To prevent
The images
From eating me up
Contemplate
Inactive
Swallow
Insanities
Disillusion
Blinded
By my own
Reflection that lives
In my metaphysical
Place
Feelings

Philosophy
Emotions
Wars
History
Sciences
Detail
God
Technology
Spirituality
Analysis
Read and then
Write
To retranscribe
The words
Sentences
Ideas
Experiences
Discoveries
Of my own
Book. Read
And recover
The thought
That sustains me
That defines

What I am
What I was
What I'll be
Words
Liberate me
From my petty
Status
As a mortal
The words
Open the doors
From the infinitely
Complex
To the infinitely
Simple.
Music of
The soul.
Sounds and rhythms
Express
To my mind
The essence of
Humor
Meditation
Peace
Humanity

Fiction
Invisible
Luxury
Origin
Ideal
Lies
Abstractions
Secrets
The idea
The odor
The taste
All the senses
Heightened
Awaiting
The feast
Until
The incomparable
Final
Satisfaction or
Frustration

Turn the last page.

H.99

SPECIAL THANX TO

✗ ✗✗✝✗✝ ✝ ✗ ✗ ✗✝✝✗ ✗ ✗ ✗✗✝

GOD the almighty one who put us with the test and
supported us during this crazy adventure, for the worse and
the best. To our ancestors and guardian angels that made
everythin' possible when nothing was possible. We call that
'Miracles of Tribulations'. To the miracles of life that bless
us with princesses and prince Lea Marie, Makeda, Jamaal. To
our families, their support & unconditional love. To all our
friends, soul mates, they'll recognize themselves.

EXTRA THANX TO

All the poets, musicians, and all actors of this project without whom nothing would have been so magic. Thanx for the trust you gave us, for your patience. Thanx for your talent. To Kasema for the 99' poetic experience. To Artemis/Triloka Records : Mitchell Markus, thanks 4 believing in the power of Words. To Thierry Planelle, To Brenda Walker, my special sister Thank U So Much. Lee & Mounir, you are the soundpillars of Echos. I will never say thanx enough. Thanx to Aliza (Shorefire) for being there from the start. To LES TRANSMUSICALES de RENNES for Echos first appearance on stage. Thanx to Bowery Ballroom and Bimbo's, places we love to perform, thanks for your ever support. To Jeff, Princesse Jeanne, Amélie Chabannes, Claire KEIM, Bams, Alexandra Boston, Professor Babacar, Mme Mvogo, Famille Mahdjoubi, Gregory Protsche, to Baïfall Human Tribe for EQUALIZING Echos' leather skin, and for the SLAM OPERA kick off. To Vibes Khameleons & Hanifah Walidah for showing the path, To Vincent Tarrière, Vicelow, Aline - Radio Nova Team, JFB, Lord Jazz, Exodus, David Ngoa & T"Toff Crew, Xuly Bët, To RESPECT Magazine, To Générations 88.2FM, To Frédérique & Studio Twin-Paris, One Soul Studio-NYC, Patrick Duval and all Musiques De Nuit Crew.

A special thought all the victims of the world's violent craziness, and for their families. Prayers and Love.
TO OUR LOST POETS : Francis Bebey, Nina Simone, Leopold Sedar Senghor, Claude Nougaro.
To all the music & poetry lovers. To all the travelers thru space and time.

LA TERRE-MÈRE /MOTHERLAND

1. Elle est née en Zambie
(Souleymane Diamanka/Mounir Belkhir/Hélène Faussart)

2. Heaven
(Chuma Hicks/Fisiwe Cook/Mounir Belkhir/Hélène Faussart)

3. Les entrailles du monde
(Anouch Adjarian/Pascale Obolo/Mounir Belkhir/Hélène Faussart)

4. Au pied de l'histoire de mon père
(Souleymane Diamanka/Mounir Belkhir/Hélène Faussart)

5. Solide
(Célia Faussart/Hélène Faussart/Jean M'Ba)

6. Freedom (Live Version)
(Takeasha Henderson/Brian Frazier Moore/Kevin Arthur)

URBAN CITY LIFE/ DANS LA VILLE

7. War in Babylone
(Jamarhl Crawford/Mounir Belkhir/Hélène Faussart)

8. Prose électrique. Part 1
(John Mitko/Lois Da Sila/Guillaume Lambert)

9. Demain (Live Version)
(Célia Faussart/Hélène Faussart/arranged by Brian Frazier Moore & Kevin Arthur)

10. NYC
(Kasema Kalifah/Mounir Belkhir/Hélène Faussart)

11. Rendez-vous Paris
(John Mitko/Lois Da Silva)

12. Rendez-vous NY
(John Mitko/Lois Da Silva)

13. Embrasse moi (Deep Wookie remix)
(Erika Dobong'na/Mounir Belkhir)

14. Prose électrique. Part 2
(John Mitko/Lois Da Silva/Guillaume Lambert)

DES HOMMES ET DES FEMMES/LOVE STORIES

15. To the Queen
(Jamarhl Crawford/Mounir Belkhir/Helene Faussart)

16. Untitled Rhapsody (Live version)
(Nazelah Jamison/Brian Frazier Moore/Kevin Arthur)

17. Je te souhaite une blanche nuit
(Souleymane Diamanka/Mounir Belkhir/Helene Faussart)

18. The Death and the Living
(Kasema Kalifah/Mounir Belkhir/Helene Faussart)

SPIRITUAL HUMAN NATURE/LES ÉLÉMENTS

19. Quand le ciel éclate en sanglots
(Souleymane Diamanka/Mounir Belkhir/Helene Faussart)

20. Fire
(Takeasha Henderson/Mounir Belkhir/Helene Faussart)

21. I disagree
(Helene Faussart/Celia Faussart)

22. La prose des Vents
(Souleymane Diamanka/Mounir Belkhir/Helene Faussart)

CREDITS ECHOS

✝ ✗ ✝ ✗ ✗ ✝ ✗ ✗ ✝ ✝ ✗ ✗ ✝ ✝ ✗ ✗ ✗ ✗ ✝ ✝ ✗ ✗

PRODUCED BY NUBIATIK Publishing LLC

EXECUTIVE PRODUCTION: Helene Faussart for NUBIATIK

MUSIC produced & arranged by
Mounir Belkhir & Helene Faussart (1,2,3,4,5,7,10,14,16,17,18,19,21)
Jean M'Ba, Helene Faussart & Celia Faussart (track 5)
Yogi & DJ Wamba pour BA-GY Structure (8,13)
DJ Wamba – VIZJONER (11)
Brian Frazier Moore & Kevin Arthur (6,9,15)
Lee Hamblin (20)
Jason 'Katt' Chue aka WOOKIE (12)

RECORDED AT
Studio One Soul – NYC
La Ka – Marseille
Upside Studio - Bordeaux
Studio Antenna – Paris
Studio Davout – Paris
Studio La Seine – Paris
Studio Vizjoner – Paris
Studio Fertile- Montmagny
Studio F1- Paris
SOUL II SOUL Studio – London
Bowery Ballroom – NYC
BIMBO's – San Francisco

RECORDED BY
Patrick Lo Re
Mounir Belkhir
Martin Polak
Kenny Nash assisted by Andre Houser
DJ Steady
Lee Hamblin
Julien Tekeyan

MIXED BY
Lee Hamblin at Studio TWIN – Paris
Assisted by Olivier
William Gouot for Studio F1

MASTERED BY
JC at TRANSLAB – Paris
Glenn Meadows for Compendia

MUSICIANS
Live tracks (6,9,15)
Drums: Brian Frazier Moore
Bass: Kevin Arthur
Guitar: Tim Motzer
Piano & Keys: Pete Kuzma
Rhodes & Keys: Junius Berzine
Backing Vocal (9): Caroline Riddick & Monique Harcum
Studio Tracks :
Flute (3) : Monet
Backing Vocal (10): Stacy King
Bass (14,16,17): Farid Khenfouf
Guitar (14,16,17) : Stephane Salerno
Guitar (5) : Jean M'Ba
Percussion & Kalimba (5) : Julien Tekeyan
Opera singer (21): Anne Malorant

TRANSLATION TRIBE
Supervisor : Célia Faussart
Pierre Martung
Emmanuelle Farine
Achta Clanet-Dubois
Melinda Herron
Daniel Kline-Dubois
Merci à tous, amoureux des mots pour ce travail titanesque

BOOK & CD ARTWORK by Richard "Reach" Mvogo
PHOTOGRAPHY by Piotr Sikora, Luc Valigny, Amélie Chabannes, Jeromine Derigny,
Helene Faussart, Pierre Bidart, Ifetayo Abdus-Salam, Baron & D.R.
ARTISTIC DIRECTION by Helene Faussart

QUOTES CREDITS :

✝✝✕✕✕✕✝✕✝ ✝✕✕✕✝✕✕✕✕✕✝

« ON DIT QUOI/SAYS WHO » Proverbs by Souleymane Diamanka
Writers/Authors :
Jacques Audinet, *Le temps du métissage* © Editions de l'Atelier, 1999
Friedrich Nietzsche. © d.r
Ralph Ellison, *Shadow and act,* © Random House
Henry James, *La bête dans la jungle,* © Edition LGF
Mumia Abu Jamal, © Plough Publishing House
Patrick Chamoiseau, Texaco, © Editions Gallimard
Ed. Gallimard.
Jacques Chevrier. *Anthologie africaine II: poésie,* Hatier 1988 © Editions Hatier International,
2002,2003, Coll. Monde Noir Poche, Editions Hatier International, 2002, Coll. Monde Noir.
Veronique Tadjo. *Latérite,* © Veronique Tadjo
The Holy Bible-La Bible.
Extrait de « New York », Ethiopiques (1956) in Œuvre Poétique, Ed. Seuil, Léopold Sedar
Senghor,© Editions du Seuil, 1964, 1973, 1979, 1984, et 1990.
Extrait de Paroles intimes, Patrice Kayo, © Editions de l'Harmattan
Extrait de Souffles tiré de Leurres et lueurs, Birago Diop
© Présence Africaine 1960.
Extrait de Fleur de Lance, Bernard Zadi Zaourou. © Editions de l'Harmattan
Extrait de Musica Africa, Francis Bebey, © Editions de l'Harmattan
Proverbs from the World Cultural Patrimony.

ECHOS NOTA

✝✝✝✕✕✝✝✕✝ ✝✝✕✕✝✝✕✕✝

We compiled, produced and mastered Echos Chapter One from January 2000 to May 2005.
Some poems might echo the latest World History pages written with bloody and devilish hands.
We decided to keep all the pieces and contents of the project
And we never intended to hurt anybody
In any way.

Those poems should be listened and read to heal and to comfort our soul, body and mind.
To pray and meditate for our families
And their beloved ones
Lost ones
Around the timeless battlefield
With the aim
And understanding that
No such things will happen again
Since Love rules our lives.
Now more than ever.

« The Creator has a masterplan... »

And it's a Love plan.
A LOVE MASTERPLAN.

H.

This book is dedicated to our beloved mother
Veronique Ngoa-Aicamba Faussart

MORE INFO ON POETS :
www.nubiatik.com

Colophon

Publisher: Raoul Goff
Art Director: Iain Morris
Executive Directors: Michael Madden, Peter Beren
Designer: Usana Shadday
Additional Graphics: Reach Mvogo
Acquiring Editor: Lisa Fitzpatrick
Managing Editors: Linda Kelly, Mariah Bear
Editorial Associate: Danny Grinberg
Production: Lisa Bartlett, Noah Potkin